INTERCONNECTING WORLDS
Teacher partnerships for bilingual learning

INTERCONNECTING WORLDS
Teacher partnerships for bilingual learning

Charmian Kenner and Mahera Ruby

Trentham Books
Stoke on Trent, UK and Sterling, USA

Trentham Books Limited
Westview House   22883 Quicksilver Drive
734 London Road   Sterling
Oakhill   VA 20166-2012
Stoke on Trent   USA
Staffordshire
England ST4 5NP

First published 2012

British Library Cataloguing-in-Publication Data
A catalogue record for this book is available from the British Library

The author and publisher wish to thank the following for their kind permission to reproduce material: Shaheen Akhter for the cover photo; Osman Ali for Figure 11, Annika Eadie for the photo in Figure 13; and the parents of the children who took part in the research for the children's writing and drawing. It did not prove possible to contact the copyright owners for Figures 5, 6 and 10, although every effort was made to do so.

ISBN 978-1-85856-512-5

Designed and typeset by Trentham Books Ltd, Chester and printed in Great Britain by 4edge Limited, Hockley

To Rakib Ahmed

*whose vision of uniting children's learning
across complementary and mainstream settings
continues to inspire us*

Acknowledgements

We would like to thank

- all the children, families and teachers for taking part in the research and sharing their ideas with us

- Jamal Uddin, Shabita Shamsad and colleagues at Tower Hamlets Languages Service for our rich collaboration over the years

- Eve Gregory and Salman Al-Azami for investigating bilingual learning with us

- the Economic and Social Research Council, Paul Hamlyn Foundation and Tower Hamlets Directorate of Children, Schools and Families for funding our work

- the excellent team at Trentham Books, especially Gillian Klein, John Stipling and Shawn Stipling

Special thanks to the complementary and mainstream schools who helped produce resources and run professional development sessions based on our research: Stifford Centre, Wadajir, Darul Ummah and Svetlyacok complementary schools, and Smithy Street Primary School.

Contents

Introduction • ix

Chapter One
Simultaneous or Separate Worlds? • 1

Chapter Two
Developing Bilingual Learning in Mainstream School • 27

Chapter Three
Sharing Strategies • 61

Chapter Four
Connecting the Curriculum • 91

Conclusion
Promoting Learning Power • 117

References • 121

Index • 127

Introduction

Rakib is teaching a group of nine-year-olds how to write double letters in Bengali. The setting is an after-school Bengali class that takes place in the London primary school classroom where Rakib is also a mainstream teacher during the day. Sitting round a table with the three children, Rakib invites them to compare the English and Bengali writing systems. He holds up a small whiteboard on which he has just written the English letter 'n', and the children supply the Bengali letter with the equivalent sound. He adds another English 'n' to make the double letter 'nn' and they sound it out together.

Then Rakib writes the double letter in Bengali, and the children note a striking difference – whereas 'nn' in English is written horizontally, the two 'n' symbols in Bengali are joined vertically. Rakib gives examples of Bengali words containing this sound, and the children recognise *ranna* which means 'cooking'. Finally, Rakib asks them to find as many examples as they can of this double letter symbol in their worksheet, and write the words on their own small whiteboards. The children set to work eagerly.

Rakib can now turn his attention to pupils seated at another table, who have been studying independently meanwhile. Each is working at their own pace through the pages of a textbook specially designed for children learning Bengali in the London context. As well as being written in Bengali script, each word or phrase is also provided in English to aid understanding. Children practise reading silently or aloud to themselves in Bengali, preparing for the moment when Rakib or his assistant teacher Shuaib arrive to check their new knowledge. Some listen to their more advanced classmates or are corrected by them.

In the last part of the class, children engage in speaking and listening activities such as making up conversations between puppets in typical South Asian dress, or shopping roleplays where they bargain over fruit and vegetables as they would in the nearby street market. Rakib finishes the session by reading a Bengali folk tale to the whole class.

This class is one of thousands taking place after school or at weekends around the UK, in which children learn about the languages and cultures of their families and communities. Such 'complementary schooling' is run by dedicated teachers – almost all volunteers, since very little funding is available. Many have qualifications from their countries of origin and some are also teachers or teaching assistants in primary or secondary schools during the day.

Children's learning in these community settings is considerable. As they engage with reading and writing in Chinese or Somali, Polish or Urdu, they gain knowledge that supports their bilingual literacy development. Many complementary teachers encourage children to compare their different writing systems. In another example from Rakib's class, he showed his pupils a recipe in Bengali and asked them to identify all the verbs used in the instructions. This led to a discussion on how word order differs from English, since verbs usually appear at the end of a phrase in Bengali. Such metalinguistic knowledge connects well to the analysis of language that children undertake in English literacy lessons.

Equally important is the opportunity for children to explore their cultural identities so they can feel at ease growing up as Bangladeshi British, for example. The children in Rakib's class studied poetry by the Bangladeshi Nobel Laureate, Rabindranath Tagore, giving them access to a rich literary heritage. They also enjoyed the chance to use familiar phrases in Sylheti, the variety of Bengali spoken in their local East London community, as they acted out dramas with puppets as mothers and aunts, or created the characters of clever market traders in their shopping roleplay. In these communicative interactions, children blended languages and cultures. English, Sylheti and Bengali co-exist and intertwine in their everyday lives.

The connections between children's Bengali and English learning are particularly evident in Rakib's class because the session took place on mainstream premises where Rakib also taught during the school day. Links between complementary and mainstream schools in the UK are now beginning to be made, encouraged by initiatives such as the government-funded Our Languages project (Our Languages, 2012) and the National Resource Centre for Supplementary Education (NRC, 2012). However, many mainstream teachers remain unaware that their pupils attend complementary schools, and hardly any of them have visited such settings. Where policymakers and teachers do not know complementary schools exist or consider them insignificant, their work is silenced and separated from the mainstream. This silence and separation is maintained by staff who teach in both settings but feel they cannot mention their after-school work to mainstream colleagues. Even the children themselves say nothing about their complementary schools. Why is this the case?

One primary school teacher in East London, who was about to participate in our action research study with complementary schools, reflected on how little she currently knew about children's out-of-school learning:

> What happens with children outside the school is very separate from us, we don't really get to see that other part of the child, and having worked particularly with the older children they often don't like to really talk to you about it ... I think they see that side of their life as much more part of their family and community, and the school – sadly, I don't know if they feel that as much.

Aware that some of her pupils attended Arabic classes, she had asked about them with interest, hoping to find out what went on there. To her surprise, children were not forthcoming, and she assumed their reticence meant they preferred to keep school and community learning as separate parts of their lives. She was keen to begin working in partnership with a complementary school teacher because 'I think it will give me a bit more of that whole picture of the children, because there's always that little bit that's missing.'

In this book we look critically at why children feel it necessary to hide such significant parts of their lives from their mainstream teachers. What are the powerful forces that make children's multilingual knowledge and identities seem so irrelevant in daytime school? Why did one of the children in our study have to say, when her primary school teacher visited her Bengali class, 'it was the first time anyone came to see us'?

Our research shows the changes that happen when mainstream educators build links with complementary schools and begin to recognise the hugely valuable work taking place there. By visiting complementary classes, mainstream teachers see the vital contribution their teacher colleagues make to children's academic and social development. By working together to create topic-based lessons that can be taught in both settings, complementary and mainstream teacher partners provide a coherent educational experience for children that fully exploits the advantages of multilingual learning. By involving parents and grandparents in curriculum work and by organising joint events between mainstream and complementary schools, educators draw on home and community knowledge and forge stronger bonds with families.

The book tells the story of two consecutive research projects on bilingual learning with teachers in Tower Hamlets, East London. Our first investigation began with primary school teachers who knew bilingualism was supposed to be an asset but were not sure if it was still relevant to children of second and third generation Bangladeshi origin, the majority group in their classes. Chapter One, Simultaneous or Separate Worlds, reveals children's own views on the important role of Bengali in their everyday lives, and their awareness of how it could contribute to their learning at mainstream school. However, when invited to use Bengali as well as English for tasks at primary school, the children initially found themselves tongue-tied, struggling to make use of their bilingual capacities. Although they were building Bengali knowledge in complementary class, primary school was a monolingual space where it was difficult to express their multilingual identities. We describe how we worked with teachers and children to overcome these barriers and develop bilingual learning.

Chapter Two, Developing Bilingual Learning in Mainstream School, shows how the first research project progressed as primary teachers devised literacy and numeracy tasks to be conducted bilingually, linking with children's home and community resources. We discuss how these activities enhanced learning, enabling children to transfer ideas between languages, enrich meaning through translation, build knowledge about how languages work, and develop new cultural understandings. Through this work children began to construct multilingual identities at school. Complementary teachers and bilingual teaching assistants helped generate new strategies that included involving parents and grandparents, creating bilingual resource material, and using transliteration as a bridge between Bengali script and English. Such learning approaches were found to be inclusive and motivating for whole-class work, whether the languages the children were engaging with were familiar or new to them.

Through this bilingual work, mainstream teachers began to understand the importance of family and community knowledge in children's lives. However, they had not yet visited complementary schools or formed full partnerships with teachers there. Our second project made this possible through collaborative action research between complementary and mainstream teachers to co-construct bilingual learning. Two primary schools participated, together with Bengali, Somali and Russian classes in their neighbourhoods. Chapter Three, Sharing Strategies, explains how teacher partners visited each other's settings, and planned topic-based lessons adapted to each context. As they worked together, they exchanged ideas on teaching approaches. Mainstream teachers discovered how complementary classes operated as learning communities in which children worked both independently and collectively. Complementary teachers gained additional knowledge of groupwork, games and roleplay. Since they already taught bilingually, they helped their mainstream partners bring the children's different languages into learning at primary school.

Chapter Four, Connecting the Curriculum, demonstrates how complementary teachers brought a holistic perspective to learning, rooted in their knowledge of children's lifeworlds outside mainstream school. The *learning power* generated when they worked with their communities in complementary school began to operate in primary school too. With their mainstream partners, the complementary teachers broadened and deepened the curriculum, involving children and their families as active contributors to investigate topics ranging from intergenerational relationships to sociopolitical issues such as global trading. Mainstream teachers also began to draw upon their own knowledge of languages and cultures. The multilingual community-based topic work engaged their personal experience in ways previously untapped in a monolingual curriculum.

In the Conclusion we reflect on how complementary and mainstream teachers can work together, giving each other mutual support to benefit all their pupils. Given the unequal power relationships in our society, efforts made by complementary teachers to contact mainstream schools often go unheeded. Mainstream educators need to reach out to complementary schools, and as visits are exchanged and joint events planned, productive partnerships develop. Children's worlds, kept separate by the exclusion of home experience from mainstream school, are finally united. Their multilingual identities are valued, and they bring together their knowledge from home, complementary class, and mainstream school. By making the connections, we enable children's learning to thrive.

1

Simultaneous or Separate Worlds?

At home we speak Bengali, then we come to school and slowly slowly we forget Bengali and then we will be like the English people only speaking one language

This is the school hall, we're not used to speaking Bengali here

The first remark was made by an eleven-year-old at an East London primary school. She recognised the language knowledge that she and her peers built up during their early years at home, and their potential to become bilingual. She realised they had lost the opportunity because learning at school took place entirely in English, and she regretted it.

The second statement indicates how Bengali comes to be forgotten. This comment was made by a nine-year-old being interviewed with a small group of classmates in another East London school where over 90 per cent of children were Bangladeshi British. The researcher asked the children their opinions about speaking Bengali at school. During our action research with their teachers, we had discovered that children felt tongue-tied when offered the chance to learn in Bengali as well as English. We needed to find out why, since we knew they commonly switched between English and Bengali in the school playground and at home. The interview took place in a corner of the school assembly hall and once again, the children seemed to find it difficult to answer in Bengali, even though they were alone with Bengali-speaking researchers. When the children tried to explain their continual use of English, one of them named the problem directly. The school hall was not a place where Bengali was normally spoken.

The teachers were alarmed to hear that children felt this way. They thought they were giving positive messages about children's home languages. However, whilst Bengali was spoken by bilingual teaching assistants to children in early years classes, the aim was to smooth the transition to English. From then on, pupils might be asked to translate for new classmates arriving from Bangladesh, but Bengali would not otherwise be used. The children told the researcher how upset they had felt when one of them was sent out of the class for speaking Bengali. Yet it turned out the teacher was unaware they had interpreted the incident in this way. She had disciplined the child for talking too much in class, and was distressed to discover that children thought it was because of the language they were speaking.

Together, the researchers and teachers began to realise that children experienced formal school spaces such as the hall or classroom as an 'English-only' zone. There was no official school policy promoting bilingualism, and no encouragement of bilingual learning as part of the curriculum. So although parents might chat in Bengali in the foyer, and teachers might learn a few words to joke with children in the corridor, teaching and learning took place only in English. Children were well aware of this institutional silence and became accustomed to compartmentalising their use of languages. Bengali was for family and community, whilst English was for school. In this way, they came to live in separate worlds.

This chapter describes how the separation of children's worlds came to light when our project on bilingual learning began. Children revealed a wealth of linguistic and cultural knowledge as they worked on bilingual tasks at primary school, yet found it difficult to make full use of these resources in the school context. We explain how, together with their teachers, we tried to address these issues and take the project forward. First we discuss children's worlds of learning in home and community settings, and why languages other than English are so often excluded from mainstream school.

Multilingual homes, monolingual schools

Research with children growing up in bilingual or multilingual contexts shows they tend to experience their linguistic and cultural worlds as connected rather than separate. This was the finding of a study by Charmian Kenner, one of the authors of this book, with London six-year-olds learning to write in Chinese, Arabic or Spanish at the same time as English (Kenner, 2004a). At home and at their weekend complementary schools, the children lived in 'simultaneous worlds', switching between languages both in speaking and writing, and producing texts that expressed their bilingual lives. Yazan and his ten-year-old sister Lana wrote together at home, starting their exercise books in English at one end and Arabic at the other. Within the pages, the two languages mingled as Yazan experimented with both. Selina produced a drawing of her mother with the Chinese character meaning 'love' above her mother's head and the English words 'I love my mum' below. Sadhana often looked for words in a bilingual dictionary with her mother and aunt, and invented her own system of spelling that linked English and Spanish sounds.

Other researchers have also found that children develop multilingual skills in their homes and communities, especially now that digital media are available in different languages. Ken Cruickshank's ethnographic study of Arabic-speaking families in Sydney, Australia (Cruickshank, 2004) showed how young people communicated with friends and family via the internet and watched films and TV in Arabic as well as English. Eva Lam and Enid Rosario-Ramos (2009) interviewed teenagers from diverse origins in the United States and found they engaged in transnational networking in multiple languages, and obtained news and information from around the world. Like the children in Charmian Kenner's UK-based study, these young people in Australia and the United States were constructing multilingual identities, constantly changing through new interactions and experiences.

Yet mainstream schools rarely recognise the wealth of multilingual knowledge and experience that children and young people possess. At the secondary schools in Cruickshank's study, families from language backgrounds other than English were generally assumed to be lacking in literacy. Young people in the research by Lam and Rosario-Ramos were aware that digital media helped maintain home languages they would otherwise lose, since English was the only language in use at school. Children in Kenner's research taught Chinese, Arabic or Spanish to classmates at primary school as part of the study, and their teachers were impressed to discover their bilingual abilities at such a young age.

Schools as institutions are part of a wider society that ignores and devalues community languages. Particularly in countries where English is the dominant first language, its global importance is emphasised, whilst languages spoken and learned by people from ethnic minority backgrounds are seen as having lesser value. Monica Heller (1995:374) has called these ideas 'monolingualising ideologies'. Such powerful ideologies permeate society and become part of school life and learning. Guadalupe Valdés and colleagues (2008:107) argue that 'hegemonic beliefs about monolingualism and bilingualism are deeply embedded in educational institutions' in the US, for example.

Since schools play a key role in socialising children and preparing them for employment, the only 'legitimate language' is the dominant one, as Pierre Bourdieu pointed out (Bourdieu, 1991). Parents and children are given to understand that possessing this 'linguistic capital' will lead to success in the job market, access to powerful social networks, and high-status knowledge and qualifications. To maintain the dominant language's position in society, other languages are continually devalued through a process of 'symbolic violence' (Bourdieu, 1991). Those who use non-dominant languages feel reproached for doing so, and gradually internalise a negative view on ways of speaking and writing that are part of home and community experience. Even a look or a comment can be enough to silence self-expression, and eventually people police themselves by not using their language in institutional contexts. Jim Cummins (2010) speaks of the 'invisible English-only sign' on the wall of many classrooms, and the children in our research project, who sensed that Bengali was not valued in school, had understood this all too well.

Breaking the silence

Our research challenged the monolingual perspective by giving children the chance to use their bilingual skills in school. At the time, educational policy in the UK was becoming more positive towards bilingualism, with statements such as 'continuing development in one's first language can support the learning of English and wider cognitive development' (DfES, 2003:31). The government commissioned new training materials on this basis (DfES, 2006), but these were not widely integrated into teacher education. So whilst teachers in London schools often told us they thought it an advantage for children to be bilingual, we found they were unsure how to use bilingual learning strategies in the classroom. Meanwhile, 'monolingualising ideologies' continued to circulate throughout the wider society. Other government ministers expressed negative opinions on bilingualism, such as Home Secretary David Blunkett's statement in 2002 that immigrants should speak English at home. There was vociferous media support in 2006 for a London headteacher who closed down bilingual science classes that aimed to improve the achievement of Turkish-origin children (Anderson *et al*, 2008). These views reinforced the idea that English was the only legitimate language for mainstream schooling.

So although the schools in our study were in Tower Hamlets, an area of East London with a long-established Bangladeshi community, children were not commonly encouraged to draw on their bilingualism for learning. However, the local education authority had a Languages Service that supported mother tongue development by funding complementary classes in Bengali and other languages. The Languages Service thought it likely that attendance at such classes contributed to educational achievement, and asked our research team to investigate. We chose to focus on Bengali, since it was the language most widely taught in local complementary schools and our team already included Bengali-speaking researchers.

In preliminary discussions with mainstream teachers, we found they were not sure how much Bengali their pupils spoke, since many families of Bangladeshi origin had been settled in London for two or three generations. Most children now seemed fluent in English, and the teachers doubted Bengali would be relevant to their learning. However, they were interested in finding out how children would respond if they had the chance to use Bengali in school, and agreed to take part in our action research project.

We decided to involve children and their teachers in two primary schools. To study bilingual learning in depth, we needed to work with small groups of children. Teachers began finding out which pupils in their classes attended complementary school. In most cases it was the first time they had asked this question. Once parents had agreed that their children could take part in the project, and children themselves had been consulted, we formed two groups in each school across a range of ages. In Primary School A, a group of four children from Year 2 (aged six to seven) and a group of five from Year 4 (aged eight to nine) took part. In Primary School B, there were another four children from Year 2, and four from Year 6 (aged ten to eleven).

By observing complementary classes, we could see what children were learning about literacy and numeracy and how much Bengali they knew. Together with the children's mainstream teachers, we then planned literacy and numeracy tasks relevant to the primary curriculum, which linked with children's knowledge from complementary school. The activities took place in various spaces in the school where it was quiet enough for the children to concentrate and be videorecorded. After each activity, we asked children to comment on how they had used Bengali and English for learning. An end of term seminar brought complementary and mainstream teachers together with the researchers, to discuss the findings so far. For the second cycle of action research, we developed the bilingual tasks further, and in a final seminar we reflected on what we had discovered. The mainstream teachers then used the knowledge they had gained to carry out whole class lessons involving bilingual learning.

Through joint work with teachers and children, we began to explore what happened when the 'monolingual silence' in mainstream school was broken, and Bengali could be used for learning as well as English. To break the silence, we had to go on a challenging journey together, which we will now explain. First we describe our starting point: children's experiences in complementary class.

Learning Bengali in complementary school

Primary School A had an on-site Bengali class after school two days a week. This class, mentioned in the Introduction, was run by Rakib, a Year 3 teacher in the school. The Year 4 group of children taking part in the project all attended Rakib's class, as did two of the Year 2 children. The other Year 2 children, and all the children in School B, attended after-school complementary classes in sites other than mainstream school: at home, in a community centre, at mosque, or an evening madrassah at an Islamic day school. In most cases they learned Arabic on some evenings in order to read the Qur'an, and Bengali on others. Bengali was also used as a mediating language in Arabic classes, to give instructions and discuss the learning.

In Rakib's class, as we saw, children were learning to read and write Bengali from textbooks specially designed for the UK. Speaking and listening were supported by dual-language storybook tapes and roleplays with puppets, and numeracy through activities such as shopping roleplays. Some work was explicitly linked with the mainstream curriculum, such as posters produced in Bengali during Healthy Eating Week.

It proved more difficult to visit the other Bengali classes the children attended. The research was taking place shortly after the tragedy of the London bomb attacks, when the media portrayed Muslims in a negative and stereotyped way. Teachers and parents were understandably reluctant to give access to classes in homes or mosques, or even in other community contexts. Fortunately, one of our researchers already knew a family in Primary School B, and she was able to videorecord a Bengali lesson taught at home by the children's grandmother. The class included children from more than one family, and Nusrat's grandmother skilfully orchestrated activities so that children from toddlers to upper primary level were all involved in reading, writing and speaking Bengali (Ruby *et al*, 2010). Work on Qur'anic Arabic was also part of the class. The textbooks came from Bangladesh and, like the poetry that children recited with the grandmother whilst they were practising their writing, were designed for religious education as well as language and literacy learning.

Most Tower Hamlets families speak Sylheti, a variety of Bengali that no longer has a written version, and Rakib used Sylheti in his class as well. He introduced children to the differences between Sylheti and Standard Bengali, the language used in books and newspapers and often heard on TV. Some families speak varieties other than Sylheti; for example, Nusrat's grandmother spoke the Noakhali variety, though she taught her little class to read and write in Standard Bengali. The children in our study showed they were aware of differences between varieties of Bengali, and adapted to the combination of languages used by their complementary teachers. Rakib used English to explain ideas to his pupils, as well as Sylheti and Standard Bengali, whilst Nusrat and her peers switched between all the different languages in their repertoire to communicate as effectively as possible. In this multilingual context, the term 'Bangla' is used in the Tower Hamlets community to cover all varieties including Standard Bengali. We use the term 'Bangla' for the same purpose in many of our discussions below.

The complementary classes we observed evidently supported the learning of language and literacy in Bengali and Arabic, and often in English too. Children were accustomed to working in different languages in these contexts, using the whole range of their linguistic resources. The variety and flexibility of multilingual learning in community settings contrasted sharply with the monolingual environment in primary school. How could children's rich language experiences become part of their lives in the mainstream classroom?

Starting points for bilingual learning at mainstream school

With the primary school teachers, we explored the ways children might begin to use Bangla as well as English for learning, through themes drawing on home and community experience. Here we describe the initial activities children undertook in small groups. Teachers explained to the children that the work would be taking place and they could speak Bangla, but did not accompany the groups at this point. They thought children might find it easier to start communicating bilingually if they had freedom to interact as a group. Members of the research team who spoke Bangla were on hand for support if needed. Children's responses to the tasks demonstrated linguistic and cultural knowledge that had previously been hidden, but also the constraints they felt about speaking Bangla in school.

Family photos and life stories

Teachers in School A suggested the children bring photos of themselves and their families, and talk with each other about the pictures. We devised a game in which children would share their photos with the group, and then turn the pictures over and mix them up. Taking it in turns to pick up a photo, they would describe it and their friends would guess who it belonged to. Finally, they would each create their own timeline by placing their photos in order to help them talk and write about their life story.

The children responded with enthusiasm. They all brought photos to school, in some cases as many as twenty. Their discussions began mostly in English, but with key terms for relatives emerging naturally in Bangla, such as *fufu* for maternal aunt. Family terms in Bangla represent exact positions in the kinship network, because great significance is attached to the extended family and each person's place within it. In English culture, this is seen as less important, so the range of vocabulary is sparse compared to the rich variety in Bangla. Children talked about *nani* (maternal grandmother), *nanu* (maternal grandparent), and *boroma* (great-grandmother). When Shawon, speaking in Bangla, said about one of his photos: 'that was my big brother when he was little', he referred to *boro bhai* (big brother) rather than his brother's name, as different terms for siblings are used within the family depending on where one is placed in age. Being an older sibling brings certain responsibilities and a code of conduct. The children also mentioned 'cousin brother' and 'cousin sister' (first cousins). These terms have been transferred from Bangla into English and demonstrate the closeness of family relationships.

Although talk in the photo sessions began in English, children were often able to repeat their comments in Bangla on request, code-switching into English for words they did not know, such as 'wooden floor' (a common aspect of London houses but rare in Bangladesh). As they became involved in the activity, children's Bangla flowed more freely, and by the time they were describing their life stories some were speaking quite fluently. One group whispered to each other before beginning to write about their lives, and later reported they had been saying 'we should write the words we can in Bangla and the words we can't in English'. However, they mostly used English, since it would have been a considerable challenge to compose in Bengali script in the time they had available.

The children's written texts shed light on the importance of family relationships and Bangladeshi culture in their everyday lives. Shawon incorporated the Bangla words *dada* (paternal grandfather) and *bari* (home) into his account, transliterated into English lettering. He referred to *dada's bari*, a concept which could not be completely translated into English, partly because of the complex kinship term and partly because a bari means a group of houses around a Bangladeshi village courtyard, not found in the UK. Naima and Tasnim also used transliterated kinship terms when writing about their families, while Miqdad wrote of one photo 'this is me, uncle, big brother, small brother and second big brother'.

Nayim demonstrated his 'simultaneous worlds' in which aspects of his Bangladeshi and English identities were combined, by including several words in Bengali script as he related the most significant experience in his recent life: witnessing the London football team he supported winning the important national trophy, the FA Cup. His account of 'My Life' (Figure 1 overleaf) was signed with his name in English and Bengali script. He found inventive ways of combining Bengali and English word order, since verbs in Bengali come at the end of the phrase. His description went as follows (Bengali script is transliterated here and followed by the English translation):

> *amar* (my) Two favourite *din asilo* (days had) (ie I had two favourite days) When arsenal won the premiership *ami ar amar abba gesi* (I and my dad went.) Highbury Arsenal shop *asilo* (was) (ie There was Highbury Arsenal shop) *ami loisi* (I bought) 1 scarf another day I went to Arsenal vs Blackburn with my dad and my *sasa* (paternal uncle) It was a fa cup semis [semi-final] and arsenal won three-0 and we went to the final and all the players were throwing there shirt then the final came and we beat man u [Manchester United] 5-4 on penalties

Nayim's drawing of the Cup itself occupied a central place in the text. Shawon's life story similarly drew together his 'simultaneous worlds' of football and family, beginning with a description of how the entire extended family visited him as a baby in hospital, and ending with his support for Manchester United, including drawings of the team's Red Devils motif.

The variety of languages present in children's lives also became visible in their accounts. Amal, aged six, wrote about the three different languages she was learning in addition to English: Urdu (her mother's language), Bengali (spoken by her father), and Arabic for reading the Qur'an. She proudly recorded the page number she had reached in each class: 'Evry Wensday and Sunday I go to udur class. I'm on the second page. I lern aribick at hom. I'm on 27. On Thursday's I go bagoly class. I'm on 6.' She demonstrated her writing of Arabic letters too. The three other children in Amal's group also showed how they could write Arabic letters, and Jameela and Junel signed their names in Bengali.

Through these texts, the children began to represent their lives more fully, including cultural aspects they would not necessarily have considered important if doing a curriculum task in English only. The large family gatherings

9

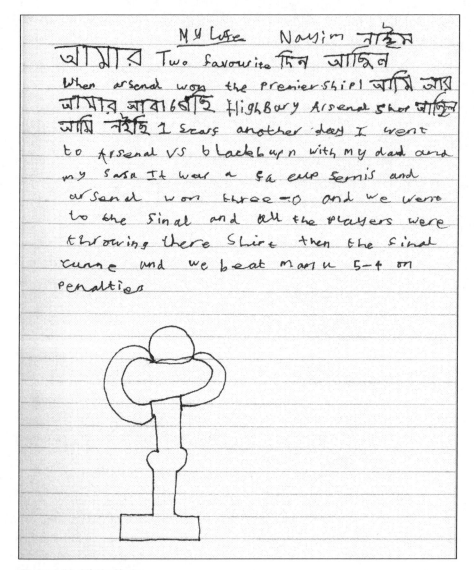

Figure 1: 'My Life' by Nayim

that typified their community were often mentioned, such as Maisha's explanation about one of her birthday parties: 'my nan's house was big enough for everyone to sit down and celebrate'. Closeknit family relationships could only be properly described through the appropriate terminology: Naima and Tasnim wrote about their birthday parties 'my dada gave me a piece of cake' and 'my 2 fufus gave 10 pounds'. Shared living with extended family is a common experience, mentioned by Miqdad: 'when my brother wasn't born my cousins used to live in my house then they went to different houses'.

Bringing a collection of family pictures to share, having time to talk about them in Bangla as well as English, and choosing how to describe 'My Life', facilitated children's sharing of their lives with each other. Reflecting on the sessions, all the children, even those less fluent in Bangla, said they enjoyed talking about the pictures in both languages. Shawon, strong in Bangla as well as English, replied that he liked using Bangla 'because I do, I just do – it's like the same', revealing the equivalent importance of both languages in his life. Although writing Bengali was considerably more difficult than speaking it, most children made efforts to do so and Nayim declared that he had wanted to include more Bengali in his text about the FA Cup.

Designing a quilt

Talking with the Year 6 teacher in Primary School B, we discovered that the children were working on the theme of quilt design in their art classes. Native American geometric patterns had been given as an example to follow by the teacher (who was Canadian), but she had not realised that quilts were commonly used and displayed in Bangladeshi homes. We agreed it would be interesting to see how children responded if given the opportunity to talk about their knowledge of Bangladeshi quilts and design their own.

A member of our research team brought a quilt she owned as an example, and all four children immediately became engaged in telling her about similar quilts in their homes. They knew the main purpose of the quilts, to keep warm in Bangladesh 'when it's a little bit cold', and other uses such as a head covering, or (in the UK) a duvet cover. Three of the four knew their quilts had been made by family members: Suraiya's mother, and Nazrin's and Iqbal's maternal grandmothers. Compared to the designs they had done in their art class, they decided the Bangladeshi quilt was more detailed and colourful. They recognised some of the iconic cultural items represented from their visits to Bangladesh. Although they needed help to remember some of the words in Bangla, they knew how each item was used. A *kolosh* was a pot to carry water on your head, drawn from the large pond (*furketun*) where people also bathe. A *fakha* was a fan that you had to spin round to cool yourself. They also reported that all their quilts at home contained a *ful* (flower) design.

The children were evidently longing to create their own designs, and each began drawing a detailed picture. These were varied and colourful, incorporating cultural motifs. Every design included a representation of the Bangladeshi flag (a red circle on green background), not usually seen on a quilt but apparently a key symbol for all the children.

Next the group were asked to interview the researcher about her quilt, in Bangla. Although they had used some Bangla in the initial informal discussion, they seemed tongue-tied when faced with a roleplay task that in the mainstream classroom would always be conducted in English. They finally found their voices in Bangla when we suggested imagining themselves on Bangla TV, and from then on they produced a stream of questions displaying genuine interest. Where had the quilt been bought, how much had it cost, did the researcher buy several of the same design, which did she like most, what would she use this one for and could she make quilts herself?

Building on the fluency generated in this discussion, the children were able to describe their own quilt designs in Bangla, prompted by the researchers when unsure of some vocabulary items. Ziaul explained that his design contained the *shapla ful* (water lily, national flower of Bangladesh), with a *nouka* (boat), *mas doroin jal* (fish net) and *dala* (rice sifter). Ziaul's choices show his awareness that fishing and rice growing are the basis of the food economy in Bangladesh. Nazrin had created stylised shapes based on typical Bangladeshi flora and fauna: fish, betel leaves and mango fruit, placed around a central water lily flower (Figure 2).

Suraiya emphasised her symmetrical placing of *shapla* flowers at each side, fish in the corners and decorated water pots in the 'middle column'. She spoke eloquently in Bangla, switching into English for terms she did not know, such as 'middle column'. In Suraiya's quilt and in Iqbal's, the Bangladeshi flag was central, whilst Ziaul used it for the corners of his pattern and Nazrin incorporated tiny flags into her free-form design. Iqbal and Ziaul each wrote BANGLA down the left hand side and DESH (homeland) down the right hand side of their designs. Together with the frequent choice of the national *shapla* flower, the flag symbols indicated children's identification with their Bangladeshi heritage.

Finally, the children wrote descriptions of their quilts as if for an exhibition. They first drew mind maps with key concepts to help their planning, in which

Figure 2: Nazrin's quilt design

Suraiya included some words in Bengali script. A relatively proficient writer in Bengali, she also code-switched into Bengali in her quilt description, for her name and the words for 'Bangladesh', 'Bangladeshi flag', 'fish', 'shapla flower' and 'water pot'. She explained she would use *lal* (red) and *shobuj* (green) for the quilt, since these are the colours of the Bangladeshi flag. The other children, though they felt unable to write in Bengali script, demonstrated cultural knowledge in their texts and a sense of personal involvement. Nazrin explained that 'there are suns in each corner because it shows how hot it is in Bangladesh', and wrote that 'the threads are placed with care'. Iqbal explained 'a dala [rice sifter] is a thing that separates the grain from the dust' and imagined that 'my quilt took 4 weeks to make, which was really hard'. Ziaul evoked his own experience in the statement: 'there is a yellow colour on the dala, which the colour of the dala really is'.

The quilt activity revealed a good deal of significant information about these children of second and third generation Bangladeshi origin. They were still able to express themselves in Bangla although they needed to switch into English for some vocabulary items. All had visited Bangladesh and felt a strong cultural affiliation for their families' country of origin. Although they found it difficult at first to conduct a classroom task in spoken Bangla, they were able to start talking if they could imagine themselves in a community-based context such as Bangla TV. And they were highly motivated to work on topics linked with experiences from home, in which they could draw on knowledge precious to them.

Suraiya was the only one of the four children who had learned to read and write confidently in Bengali script. She was also the acknowledged star of her Year 6 class. An interesting pattern began to emerge in our research. In our small sample from both primary schools, the children who were achieving highly in mainstream school turned out to be relatively fluent in Bengali and becoming literate in Bengali script too. Bilingualism and biliteracy were certainly not holding them back, and seemed likely to be contributing to their intellectual development. Shawon, aged nine, read Bengali newspapers with his aunt, who explained the meaning of difficult words to him. Naima could do maths problems in Bengali as well as English. However, their primary school teachers had known none of this. In fact, Suraiya's teacher commented before the research began: 'She's so fluent in English, she's like a native speaker or better – I wonder what her Bengali is like?'

Puppets and plays

An activity undertaken by the Year 2 group in Primary School B showed that using Bangla could aid self-expression for children who had some difficulties in their mainstream class. The group included Maryam, who found literacy tasks in English hard, although she enjoyed any chance for roleplay or acting in class. Together with classmates Raihan and Fahmida, she began an activity about directions from one place to another, which their teacher suggested because it linked with a current curriculum topic.

The researchers asked the children to explain to each other how they would get from their home to a variety of places that figured in their everyday lives such as primary school, Bengali class, Arabic class, the mosque, or the supermarket. We provided a street map of the school area and large sheets of paper for children to draw maps if they wished. Puppets were also available in case they wanted to roleplay the journeys involved.

The group engaged with the map activity for a short while, the children giving each other directions mainly in English. Was this because they did not know the Bengali terms for left and right, or felt shy about using them? Later we discovered they did know the words, but were accustomed to using English for such tasks in school. However, Maryam soon began playing with the puppets, saying 'Let's go to Bangladesh', and the session came alive as her classmates joined in, using their puppets to converse in Bangla.

The action then moved to films, a significant part of children's everyday experience since Bollywood as well as English films are popular in the Tower Hamlets Bangladeshi community. Maryam asked 'who wants to watch Bangladesh film?' and everyone showed enthusiasm. Although Maryam began in English, saying 'hello mate, what you doing?', a reminder from one of the researchers about it being a Bangla film caused actor and audience to burst out laughing. Maryam began again, 'once upon a time...' More laughter ensued and she switched to '*Ekhdin...*' ('one day', the classic beginning to a story in Bangla).

From this point onwards Maryam demonstrated considerable eloquence in Bangla. She introduced different characters, roleplaying a dialogue between husband and wife with extravagant gestures and dramatic changes in tone of voice that were reminiscent of a romantic scene from a Bollywood film. The watching children became animated and involved. Then she incorporated one of the animal puppets into the story, inventing an energetic episode where Fahmida used the spider puppet to frighten one of the characters. This reminded Maryam of Spiderman, a cartoon character familiar to all the children, and she switched into English, saying 'Let's play Spiderman game'. Thus Bollywood and Hollywood culture mixed in the session, as they would do in children's home lives, until Maryam announced 'I thank you to be quiet, eat your popcorn'.

Finally, Maryam sang a Bollywood style song in Hindi, the language most often used in Indian films. She made her puppet kiss Fahmida's, saying in English 'kiss me baby', 'you're getting married' and 'I love you – end of story – I'm done', much to the amusement of Raihan and Fahmida. When the children discussed the session later with the researchers, they asked to see the film and song sequences again on the videorecording, and watched with enjoyment, eagerly anticipating the best lines. Fahmida commented on Maryam's performance: 'it was a funny show ... she sang some beautiful songs'. All agreed it was easier to talk about the film in Bangla, though Maryam's code-switching into English at key moments was appreciated. As Fahmida noted: 'I like when she said kiss me baby, her voice was funny'.

Fahmida told a story based on Maryam's film, in which a girl was frightened by a bee and a spider. Encouraged to retell it in Bangla, she first hesitated but then was able to do so, apart from the words 'spider', 'sting' and 'pretty please' which she included in English. Raihan followed with his own story in Bangla, which he could also translate fluently into English. Inspired by Maryam's Bollywood film scene, his story involved a girl who saw a man she wanted to marry, asked her mum for permission and was told she could marry anyone she wanted, so 'she lived with him for everyday'. Raihan had clearly enjoyed the session and stated: 'I want to come again'.

In answer to questions from the researchers, the children explained they spoke English and some Bangla at home and no Bangla at school, where it was 'not allowed, because some teachers don't understand what we say'. However, they would speak Bangla with friends in the playground. On rewatching extracts from the videorecording, they began discussing several home-related aspects of their lives, from Eid celebrations to eating fish at Bangladeshi weddings in London. When asked if they would usually talk about these subjects at school, Raihan smiled and answered 'I talk about it in here', meaning in the room where the session was taking place. Asked if he could talk about it in the classroom, he said 'no – but I tell my friends in the playground'.

This session offered an illuminating glimpse into children's bilingual lives. Whilst the directions task did not prompt them to use Bangla, apparently since they were not used to doing so for classroom work, the puppet roleplays helped them make links to home experiences where Bangla was commonly used. We discovered Maryam's impressive powers of self-expression in Bangla, which went well beyond her current knowledge of spoken English. Her lengthy stories were a potential stimulus for writing in English, since children often find it easier to compose when they have first generated ideas through speaking. Her eloquence and her varied narratives were also a catalyst for Fahmida and Raihan to tell stories in Bangla, revealing a knowledge of the language we had not suspected at first.

We were also struck by children's feeling that they could not speak Bangla at school, other than in the playground. Raihan's comment that he could not talk about aspects of his home life in the classroom was another matter of concern. Where were these prohibitions, as children interpreted them, coming from? If the research project was to progress, we needed to investigate further.

Exploring children's views on using Bangla at school

All four groups of children expressed similar opinions when we asked them whether they preferred working in Bangla, in English or in both languages. Having had the opportunity to undertake activities bilingually, they said they preferred using both. Whilst most felt English was their stronger language, they wanted to use Bangla as well. For example Nusrat, aged five, said she felt it was easier to do a task in both languages 'because we get to speak in Bangla *and* English', and her classmate Fahmida added 'yes, that helps us to speak English and Bangla'.

The Year 4 group who worked on the family photo activity chorused 'Yes!' when asked if it was easier to talk in both languages. Naima explained she found it an advantage 'because if you don't understand a word in English, somebody can just say what it means and think of it in Bangla and just add that word to the sentence'. This comment, from a child who was achieving highly in English, suggested that drawing on resources from both languages enhanced her learning.

The children also concurred in feeling that Bangla was not generally used at school. Comments by the group who did the puppet activity were mentioned above. Children doing the family photo activity seemed unsure when asked if they spoke Bangla at school, but eventually said they did so in the playground and sometimes in the classroom, 'with friends'. It seemed Bangla was not recognised as a language for learning. Children doing the quilt activity spontaneously commented on this when chatting as they coloured in their designs. One said with feeling: 'why can't we speak Bangla in class?'

The teachers were concerned when they heard about the children's comments and agreed it was important to discuss the issues in more depth. So it was decided that the Bengali-speaking researchers would talk with each group, to explain more clearly what the research was about and ask children what aspects of home and community knowledge they would like to share with their teachers. The group discussions revealed why children thought they were participating in the project. Those who attended Rakib's after-school Bengali class at their primary school saw the bilingual activities as an extension of that class, whilst others also stated they had come 'so we can learn more Bangla'. They were aware they needed to develop their knowledge of Bangla, especially in terms of literacy; some of the children who wrote about their quilt design said they could write 'a little bit' but not enough to express those particular ideas. When asked if they would do anything differently if they undertook the same activity again, they all said 'yes, write more Bangla!'

The children seemed to use Bangla at home to varying degrees. Several explained they spoke Bangla mainly with their fathers; it is quite common for women who have grown up in the Tower Hamlets community to marry men who come from Bangladesh. One child was in the rare situation of having two parents who were the first generation to arrive in England, and commented 'you have to talk to your parents in Bangla, cos if you speak English they won't understand'. Some parents actively encouraged the use of Bangla: 'if someone speaks English in your home your dad says 'why don't you say in Bangla?''. One mother seemed to discourage code-switching ('my mum says not to – she says a little bit English and a little bit of Bangla doesn't make sense'), though it was not clear whether this meant focusing only on one language or the other. Another mother definitely wanted her child to grow up bilingual:'my mum wants me to learn half English and half Bangla'.

The children felt generally positive about being bilingual. They experienced it as an advantage in translating for people in the community: 'if someone came up to you and didn't understand English it's a good thing that you can understand English and you know what they say'. Bangla was also useful in communicating with the wider world, for example 'if you're writing a letter to somewhere else' or 'if you go to Bangladesh and they can't speak English like us'. One child demonstrated their emotional affiliation to the language by stating simply: 'it's your mother tongue'.

According to the children, their Bengali and Arabic classes had relatively flexible rules about operating bilingually. Even if teachers did not speak much

English themselves, they allowed pupils to use English and would ask them to translate what they were saying. In mainstream school, the story was rather different. Only one child remembered a teacher asking a class to speak in different languages. Otherwise, the story of only being allowed to speak English in class was repeated. Children were sensitive to the needs of teachers and classmates, realising that 'English people don't understand' or that although 'some children don't mind – some think we're talking about them'. Children in one group reported that their teacher sometimes asked 'can you say that word in Bangla?' and that 'we help her – she doesn't know Bangla'. However, another child in the same group stated 'we're not allowed to speak Bangla', so there seemed to be a sense of a wider prohibition throughout the school.

Speaking Bangla in school was associated with covert or transgressive behaviour. When asked if they could use Bangla, children in one group said 'when we're doing work we don't talk – sometimes we whisper' and began referring to other instances where language use was considered unacceptable, such as swearing at playtime. Another group, who thought teachers could not hear them talking Bangla in the playground, reported using it to tell secrets. And another group said they would use Bangla at breaktime, but hardly ever in class because they thought they would be sent out of the room. They gave several examples of incidents where this seemed to have been the reason for a child being disciplined, and felt it was very unfair. They thought it was wrong to assume that Bangla was being used to say bad things, when it could be used for a variety of different purposes: 'we can say so many things'. One child asked 'why should we be thrown out of the class if we don't say anything bad?' Apparently, because Bangla was not officially encouraged for learning, the language was either silenced altogether or became an issue of contention between teachers and children.

The children did however have many positive ideas about what they could do if enabled to work bilingually. Looking at the class workbooks they had brought to the discussion, they suggested translating poetry from English into Bangla, doing maths in Bangla, writing a diary entry in Bangla or a letter of complaint to a restaurant. They thought they would like to share stories they knew with their teachers, particularly about experiences they had had in Bangladesh ('we could talk about Bangladesh when it's night!'), or faith stories such as those about Prophet Muhammad. They were excited about interacting with their teachers in this way, although some expressed initial anxiety that they hoped to get over: 'I'm not brave enough to speak Bangla to [my teacher]'.

One group thought 'we're gonna be expressing our culture' and looked forward to explaining to their teacher about Bangladeshi food and clothes, 'how our *bari* (village compound) looks like, words like *dala* (rice sifter) and she'll get to know what it means'. They felt it would be 'fun' and 'different' to work bilingually. And another child commented that if this sharing took place, their teacher 'will understand us more and won't throw any of us out of the class when we speak Bangla'. Her remark poignantly expressed the children's desire for a new kind of relationship with their teachers, based on a fuller recognition of their bilingual identities.

Encouraging Bangla in school

Teachers were aware that children communicated bilingually in the playground. As one commented, 'you hear them switching to and fro all the time ... it's amazing ... they put a Bangla word in the middle of a sentence, or one child asks a question in Bangla and the other one answers in English'. None of the teachers involved in the project would forbid the use of Bangla in the classroom. One had learned a few words such as *bala* (good) to praise children, or *shesh* (finished) to ask if a task was completed. Several asked children to translate from time to time, when a classmate needed help to understand instructions. However, none was explicitly encouraging Bangla as a tool for learning. They felt uncertain about languages other than English being used in class, worrying that children might be making negative comments about them or about classmates. They also thought children who did not know Bangla (who were in a minority) would feel excluded if it was spoken. Both these reasons were understood by the children, as we have seen.

At the project seminar held at the end of the first term, researchers and teachers discussed the difficulties children were having in using Bangla for learning. The seminar group decided that children should be given the opportunity to talk about their feelings with the researchers, as described above. Teachers also realised they needed to make greater efforts to emphasise their support for bilingual learning. In the next stage of the project, teachers became more involved in planning tasks, giving instructions and interacting with children during and after the task. They reminded them: 'It's good to speak in....' and the children completed the phrase with 'Bangla!' One teacher made signs saying 'Speak Bangla!' and 'Can you think about it in Bangla and explain it in English?'

As part of the work in the second term, one group of children produced a display for the school hall on the advantages of learning Bangla. This enabled them to explore their own experiences more fully through the process of creating the display and made their knowledge of Bangla visible within the school. The group first had a brainstorming session with the support of their teacher and the help of a teaching assistant who spoke Bangla. Writing their ideas on large sheets of paper, they produced mind maps about where, why and how they learned Bangla, what they learned and who with. All of them attended Rakib's after-school Bengali class and on the previous day they had interviewed Rakib on these issues and gone on to interview their parents that evening. The interviews provided a springboard for children's thinking about the topic.

The teacher helped the children devise questions for the interviews. A big smile broke out on Naima's face when she heard they would be doing some work about Bengali class. Questions for Rakib, the children's Bengali teacher, included: how Bangla classes in London had changed over time; why he thought it important to attend; why he used English as well as Bengali in Bangla class and whether he used both in his Year 3 mainstream class. Rakib discussed several aspects of bilingual learning with the children, including his flexible use of Bangla and English to best support different pupils in Bengali class and mainstream class. He pointed out that Bengali was an additional re-source for learning, since 'Bangla can make you more confident in your main school subject if you find it hard in English'.

The questions for parents set out to explore why they thought it was impor-tant for their child to go to Bangla classes; whether the parent themselves had attended, and if not, whether they wished they had; whether they enjoyed going at the time or 'now are you glad you went?'; how often they attended, how they learnt and what they found most difficult to learn. These questions were designed for parents who had grown up in London and took into account the possibility that they might have resisted learning Bengali as chil-dren but recognised the advantages later on. With Rakib's help, the children translated the questions from English into Bengali script. Interviews showed most parents had studied Bangla in the UK at complementary class, whilst one had grown up in Bangladesh. Parents had generally enjoyed their classes, though one did so only 'sometimes' but appreciated them in retrospect. All emphasised a desire for their children to learn the language.

Children became keenly involved in talking about their ideas and recording them on the mind map posters. Comments on the **Where** poster ranged from home and community sites where they encountered the language – 'I read my auntie's Bengali newspapers' and 'on the Whitechapel stalls [local street market] they speak Bangla' – to a child's individual use of Bangla for learning in mainstream school: 'when I do maths in class I think about it in Bangla and write in English'.

The **When** poster produced a similar range of situations, from celebrations such as New Year's Eve in Bangladesh to Eid at the mosque or weddings in London, at funfairs, or simply 'Bangla is around us' or 'on the street'. Again, comments were made about school learning as an occasion for using the language: 'translating a hard word into Bangla' and 'when I'm thinking I talk Bangla to see if it makes sense'. The time for using Bangla stretched into the future: 'Bangla is going to help us for the rest of our lives'.

The poster focusing on **Who** elicited that family members, including parents and grandparents, wanted the children to learn Bangla. Children also noted that their after-school class was popular: 'lots of people come to Bangla class because it is very important for us'. They recorded **What** activities they used in the class: poems, games, making Eid cards, puppet shows, and reading 'Books 1-7' (the series of workbooks designed for children growing up in London). They were also aware that the class taught the Standard language and that: 'we can learn the other sort of Bangla'.

The **Why** poster produced a wide range of answers. Some concerned family communication: 'so we can talk to our relatives', 'if my mum knew only Bangla and I only knew English we can't share our love', and 'I can teach my brother or sister Bangla'. Others emphasised the cultural significance of Bangla: 'it helps us to talk more of our culture' or 'so you can speak your mother tongue'. One child pointed out the flexibility of bilingual interaction: 'you can speak Bangla if you get stuck in English'. With the help of the teaching assistant, children also articulated the value of being bilingual: 'career wise it will help you' and 'if you know English and Bengali, you feel clever and proud'.

Each child took responsibility for a particular part of the display, focusing on the material gathered in one of the posters. Maisha's piece on 'Where Do You Read Bangla?' (Figure 3) is an example. Maisha managed to write the title in Bengali script as well as English, even though she found Bengali literacy diffi-cult. Her description demonstrates how Bangla surrounded her in different areas of life, such as community classes, TV (including *natox* or cartoons on Channel S, a locally-based channel for the Tower Hamlets Sylheti community) and newspapers. Maisha also mentions important reasons for learning the language, including intellectual advantages and cultural ones. Her text en-capsulates different aspects of a child's bilingual life.

কই আমার বাংলা পারি ?

Where Do You Read Bangla?

Sometimes you can learn Bangla in Arabic
classes. It is held in a community centre.
Some newspapers have Bangla writing in
them. There are Bangla natox on Channel S.
You can use Bangla while you're thinking.
You can think Bengali in your head and write
in English in your book. You can speak
Bengali to your friends and relatives and
teach your little brothers and sisters.
There are Bengali programmes on TV.

By Maisha

Figure 3: 'Where do you read Bangla? by Maisha

The other children produced similarly thoughtful pieces, making creative use
of the ideas they had brainstormed together, and also the interviews with
their parents and Rakib. Their work was made into an attractive display for
the school assembly hall, and the children proudly had their photo taken
alongside it with their teacher. The group had come a long way in terms of
self-confidence about their bilingual capabilities. The school hall, previously
a place where they felt unable to speak Bangla, was now a site where they
could display their knowledge.

This example shows how teachers can begin to address the separation of
children's home and school worlds. If English is treated as the only significant language in school, children will try to construct monolingual identities. Children of second and third generation origin tend to be fluent in
English and will perform these identities with particular competence, con-
cealing their other linguistic and cultural resources. However, if teachers give

importance to community-based learning, and involve families and complementary teachers in academic work, this helps children 'live in simultaneous worlds' at school as well as in their out-of-school lives. Instead of
hiding their wider knowledge, they will see it as an asset. In this way, children's bilingual or multilingual resources become visible and can be drawn
upon to enhance their learning. In the next chapter, we discuss how children
began to use and develop these resources in school through the research
project, as they engaged in a fuller exchange of ideas with each other and
their teachers.

Ideas for making school a multilingual space

■ Consider whether there is an invisible 'English-only' sign on the wall
of classrooms in your school. Many schools take initial steps signalling
interest in languages, yet children know multilingualism is marginal
in the curriculum. The school may have a welcome poster in different
languages and a world map showing where pupils are from, but are
children comfortable with using their languages for learning? There
may be an annual event celebrating different languages and cultures,
but is multilingual work regularly on show in assembly? If not, children may feel their multilingual selves are not completely welcome in
school.

■ To find out about children's multilingual capacities, you could start
with a language survey in your class or school. Children can represent
their language interactions by drawing themselves in the centre of a
page surrounded by names of the people they communicate with
(family members, complementary teachers etc). Arrows to and from
each person can show the language/s they speak to the child and the
child speaks to them. Even young children can use different colours
along each arrow to indicate approximately what amount of time
they speak each language with each person (for example, red along
half the line shows 50% of time in Urdu, whilst blue along the other
half shows 50% in English). This Languages Chart was originally developed by Raymonde Sneddon of the University of East London and
is available on the Goldsmiths Multilingual Learning webpages at:
http://www.gold.ac.uk/media/Family_languages_chart.pdf

Monolingual children in the class can join in by showing any languages they have heard from classmates, TV, internet or on holidays.
It is often surprising to find how many languages children are aware
of in their everyday environment.

- The Languages Chart also contains a table where children can record the complementary classes they attend and whether they read and write in different languages. You can invite children to bring books and work from complementary school to show the rest of the class and put on regular display. When children receive certificates or prizes at complementary school, you can recognise their achievements at assembly.

- You can develop a dialogue with children and parents about the advantages of bilingualism. Your positive attitudes as a school or teacher carry a great deal of weight with families who may be receiving negative messages from the wider society. Useful information can be found in the FAQs about bilingualism at: http://www.gold.ac.uk/media/FAQs_on_bilingualism.pdf

  And a leaflet for parents in English or other languages is on the National Literacy Trust website at: http://www.literacytrust.org.uk/assets/0000/0282/bilingual english.pdf

  The school can underline its support through a Languages Policy explicitly promoting multilingualism and stating how it is used in learning.

2
Developing Bilingual Learning in Mainstream School

Why We Speak Bangla?
By Naima

We speak Bangla because it is our mother tongue.

When we go to Bangladesh we speak Bangla to our relatives.

As well as that, we know two languages and that makes us proud and clever.

If you talk too much English then you will start forgetting Bangla.

It's very important for us to go to Bangla class.

Bangla is not very hard when you get the hang of it.

Bangla will help career wise. You will also feel part of the culture.

If you try and talk Bangla as much as you can then you will get better.

KEEP TRYING TO SPEAK BANGLA!

This was nine-year-old Naima's contribution to work produced with her primary school classmates on learning Bangla. Naima emphasises the centrality of Bangla to her cultural identity, and the educational advantages of being bilingual. She also provides a first-hand report of how it feels to be in the front line, fighting to develop as a bilingual learner in a society with little support for languages other than English. Her final injunction 'Keep Trying to Speak Bangla!' in bold capital letters is a rallying call to her peers.

In Naima's text we find traces of her discussions with other bilingual speakers. She had interviewed her mother and written down her comment 'It's very important for my daughter to go to Bangla classes to learn and write Bangla. It is our mother tongue'. Naima re-voiced this as the opening sentence of her piece. She had also interviewed her Bengali class teacher, Rakib, about reasons for learning Bangla and noted the idea that 'when we go to Bangladesh we can talk back'. Here she points out the advantage of being able to communicate with relatives. Parvin, a teaching assistant who spoke Bangla, had asked Naima and her classmates how they felt about speaking Bangla, and together they had generated the response 'proud and clever', which Naima put into her text. The children, their families and the bilingual teaching staff spoke with a concerted voice when given the opportunity to express their views on bilingualism.

Naima's ideas about the importance of bilingual learning are strikingly similar to the findings of research. Studies have found that being bilingual does 'make you clever', because you can transfer ideas between languages and find out more about how languages work. Researchers have also shown that different cultural experiences lead to different kinds of knowledge, so being able to draw on a variety of experiences enhances your learning as well as helping you 'feel part of the culture'. Academic and cultural knowledge will both 'help career wise', through higher educational achievement and by developing skills to relate to multilingual and multicultural communities. Finally, valuing your home language as your 'mother tongue' and being proud of it gives confidence and self-esteem, underpinning your identity as a successful learner.

In this chapter we consider theoretical ideas on bilingual learning and discuss our own research findings. We were particularly interested in how bilingual learning could take place in classrooms where many children have different languages, and how children from second and third generation bilingual backgrounds would respond.

Our research questions were these:

- ▦ In what ways do children draw on linguistic and conceptual knowledge from each of their languages to accomplish bilingual learning?
- ▦ How are children's identities as learners affected by using their home language as well as English in the classroom?

Through involving mainstream teachers, bilingual teaching assistants and complementary teachers, we also wanted to investigate:

- ▦ How can bilingual and monolingual educators help children to develop bilingual learning strategies?

Although many children have complex multilingual experience, we mainly use the term 'bilingual' since our research concerns children who use at least one language other than English in their everyday lives. Their fluency in these languages, and their knowledge of reading and writing, will vary but their worlds will be very different from those of children who encounter other languages in more limited ways, for example as a school subject or on holiday. Thus the key difference is between being monolingual or bilingual, and the term 'bilingual' can for our purposes include 'multilingual'. Our focus is on how children can make use of their varied linguistic and cultural knowledge in their learning. We also consider it vital to extend the benefits of bilingual learning to children whose experience is largely monolingual, and later in the chapter we explain how teachers devised whole-class lessons showing this to be possible.

Key aspects of bilingual learning

We have identified five main areas in which research shows benefits for bilingual learners:

- *conceptual transfer*: if you know a concept in one language it helps understand a similar idea in another language
- *translation and interpretation*: when translating between languages you find subtle differences in meaning that enrich your understanding
- *developing metalinguistic skills*: you discover similarities and differences in how languages work
- *building cultural knowledge*: you learn more by drawing on a range of cultural experiences that you can compare and contrast
- *building learner identities*: you will feel more confident as a learner if the multilingual and multicultural aspects of your identity are recognised

We now explain these areas in more detail, giving examples from our research.

Conceptual transfer

Bilingual learners have the advantage of being able to pool ideas gathered from both their languages. This enables you – as bilingual – to understand words in a new language more quickly. For example, if you are learning about circulation of the blood in a science class, a good starting point is a list of keywords in your first language as well as English. A diagram with the heart, veins and arteries labelled in English or in both languages will also help considerably, supported by a bilingual dictionary where you can search for additional terms you need. If you discuss the topic with a bilingual classmate or member of staff, you can develop your ideas in first language and this acts as a springboard for discussion or writing in English.

Nancy Lemberger (2002) gives examples from a US secondary school science class in which some pupils had Russian as a first language and received support from a Russian/English bilingual teacher. The students learned rapidly as they connected existing knowledge in Russian with new vocabulary in English. This is why many local authority services in the UK have developed multilingual vocabulary resources that schools can use to support learners of English as an Additional Language, some of which are available on the internet (NALDIC, 2012a). Some schools encourage pupils to work with bilingual 'talk partners' so they can use both languages to take their learning forward. Yangguang Chen and Eve Gregory (2004) show how Chinese children in a London primary classroom accomplished a task through 'bilingual exchange teaching', combining their ideas in English and Cantonese.

Jim Cummins (2001) has explained the bilingual learning process by using the metaphor of a 'dual iceberg'. The twin peaks appearing above the surface represent the knowledge in each language, whilst there is a large area of the iceberg concealed below where the languages are interconnected in the child's mind. Cummins calls this interconnected knowledge 'common underlying proficiency'. This is where ideas can transfer between languages. The iceberg metaphor suggests that transfer occurs at a deep cognitive level. The challenge for researchers is to find ways in which transfer can be made visible, and this is why we decided to work with small groups of children who could discuss their learning in greater detail. We also wanted to know if transfer still operates usefully for children who are already using at least two languages in their lives, such as Bangla and English. In this case neither language is completely new, but there are rich possibilities for two-way or multiple transfer between them.

Mathematics across languages
We found the understanding of a concept can transfer not only when learning a new language but also when children are working with two languages already familiar to them. One striking example came when a group of Year 2 children were working on numeracy. Teachers had told us that children find it difficult to understand 'word problems', which describe an imaginary situation in which a calculation has to take place. An example of such a 'wordy maths problem' is highlighted by the Collaborative Learning Project (Collaborative Learning, 2012):

Gregory, a Tudor doctor, needs six leeches to draw enough blood out of each patient. He has thirty nine leeches in his jar. How many patients can be bled successfully?

The cultural context of the activity and the vocabulary used may be so unfamiliar that children cannot follow what is happening. In order to tackle the task, you first have to find the mathematical information wrapped up in the description. You then have to decide what kind of operation you need to use: addition, subtraction, multiplication or division. All this is particularly hard for children learning English as an additional language. If the problem was presented in numbers only, they would be able to solve it much more easily. But since numeracy tests in the UK commonly include word problems, teachers have to find ways of helping their pupils understand them.

We agreed with the teachers to make two changes in how word problems were presented. The first was to devise problems based in experiences familiar to children from their everyday lives, so they would recognise the vocabulary and could imagine themselves participating in the activities described. The second was to encourage children to work bilingually so they could make maximum use of their ideas in both Bangla and English.

We remembered the animated discussion between Maryam, Nusrat and Raihan about eating fish at Bangladeshi weddings, which arose from one of the initial research activities. Large-scale weddings are important celebrations in the lives of Bangladeshi Londoners and often involve hundreds of relatives and friends. We decided to place our word problems in this setting. We asked questions such as how many cars would be needed to take a large family to the wedding, and how many fish were needed to divide between a certain number of guests.

The children became very engaged. When they were working out how many fish they needed to feed twenty people if each fish fed four, most of the initial discussion was in Bangla. Maryam suggested drawing fish on the board. This helped the children visualise the problem, and by drawing lines to divide each fish picture into four, they found the answer. They were asked to identify which mathematical operation they were using. Fahmida was unsure, but when prompted with the Bangla word *baita* (sharing), she immediately pointed to the symbol for division. After doing so, she promptly recalled the term in English.

The idea of sharing, experienced in Bangla in familiar contexts such as a wedding, helped Fahmida understand the mathematical concept of division. The word *baita* became linked with the word 'division' in English. The children continued by making up their own word problems, using both languages, and Fahmida referred again to *baita*. This shows how mathematical concepts can be understood more deeply by thinking in more than one language.

Translation and interpretation

Translating between languages is a challenging and fascinating task. Words often do not correspond exactly and you have to work out the nearest possible meaning. This involves trying out a range of alternative interpretations and as you do so, you extend your understanding. Danielle Moore (2002) gives a good example from an Italian/French bilingual classroom. Children were comparing two words they thought might have the same meaning: *grano* in Italian and *graine* in French. Although these concepts are related, they are not exact equivalents (*grano* means grains of rice or wheat, whereas *graine* means seeds). The teacher discussed these meanings with children by talking bilingually and explaining that *graine* corresponds more closely to the word *seme* in Italian. Moore suggests that this bilingual discussion highlighted subtleties in meaning, and led to 'enriched conceptualisation' because children had to think more deeply about how grains and seeds were interrelated yet different. In our study, we were interested in finding out how children used both their languages to explore meanings that were linked but could not be translated straightforwardly.

Fairy tale similes

We found that the children were sensitive to nuances of meaning in Bangla and English. They would go beyond direct translation to seek the most appropriate term in the other language. Seven-year-olds Raihan, Nusrat and Maryam demonstrated this when translating from a Snow White storybook in Bengali that their class teacher Sarah had asked them to work on together.

As they turned the pages of the storybook whilst listening to the accompanying audiotape, the children were particularly interested in the 'Mirror, mirror on the wall' rhyme. It was signalled by dramatic music and declaimed in a threatening tone, fitting the picture of an alarming mask-like face appearing to the wicked queen as she gazed into the mirror. The children leaned over the book at this point, immersed in the poetic flow of words. Maryam explained to Sarah that 'when it says *aina aina*, that's mirror mirror'.

The children started to pick up more words in the rhyme, and chose this part of the story to write in Bengali when Sarah invited Nusrat's grandmother – who taught a home-based Bengali class attended by Nusrat – into school to work with them. Sarah asked the grandmother to help the children write the rhyme 'Mirror, mirror' in Bengali script, which they proudly did with her support. They also wrote a transliteration into Roman script below each line. Then came the challenge of translating the rhyme into English and writing their own versions.

The Bengali poem used similes to describe Snow White as having 'lips as red as blood', 'hair as black as night' and 'a body white as snow'. Nusrat, Fahmida and Raihan translated the similes themselves and discussed how to say them in English.

Children:	the lips are red like blood and her hair is black like
Nusrat:	*sul kalo rater*, like the dark
Grandmother:	*rater ondokarer moto tar sul* (her hair is like the darkness of the night)
Sarah:	aah very good description isn't it?

The children agreed on 'lips red as blood', and talked about whether to say 'hair as black as night' or 'as dark as night'. Raihan suggested the word 'skin' rather than 'body' for 'white as snow', showing sensitivity to the appropriate word in English. Raihan's version of the rhyme is shown in Figure 4. Writing in transliterated Bengali and English, he says of Snow White 'her lips are red as blood' and 'her skin is like snow'. For the other simile, which would usually be 'black as night' in English, Raihan decided on an alternative translation:

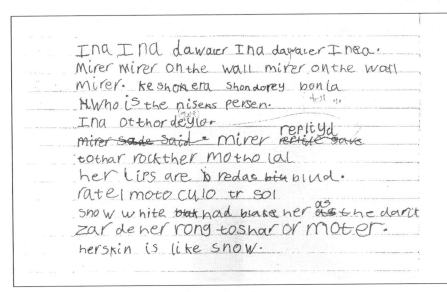

Figure 4: Raihan's version of Mirror, mirror on the wall

'Snow White had black hair as the dark', a poetic combination of ideas from Bengali and English. Thus by engaging in translation with the support of a teacher from their community as well as their mainstream teacher, the children creatively explored similes and increased their powers of literary expression in both languages.

Enriching mathematical thinking

Concepts such as age and time may be expressed differently between languages, so drawing on both systems can aid learning. Children can find it difficult to link the idea of 'half past seven' with 'seven and a half years old' in English. However, Bangla uses the same word to express the concept of 'half' in each case, with an additional term to indicate age or time. So the word *share* means 'half'; if you add *bosor*, it relates to age and when you use *ta*, it means time.

Nazma, a bilingual teaching assistant at School B, pointed out the connections in Bangla and offered to lead a maths activity with the Year 2 group to show the links between 'half' and 'half past'. She planned a lesson that presented the concepts step by step, relating the discussion to children's own experience. Their class teacher Sarah was also present and began by reminding them of another recent task where they had used time lines in class. Nazma drew a horizontal line showing numbers from one to twelve and the children found the numbers on a cardboard clock face. They practised the numbers in Bangla, and Nazma recorded their age by writing their names next to the number 7 on the line. She then told them in English that her son was four and a half, and asked where he should be placed in the number line. Fahmida immediately made the connection with the clock, pointing at it to show that he would be between 4 and 5. Together, the children identified where four and a half would be in the number line.

Then Nazma asked if anyone knew how to say four and a half in Bangla, but none of the children did. So she introduced *share sair bosor* and explained that half past four would be *share sairta*. The words *share* (half) and *sair* (four) were the same for both. To show you were talking about age, you added *bosor*, and to show time, you added *ta*. She checked the children's understanding using a different example of half past two compared to two and a half, code-switching into English to highlight the concepts of age and time:

Nazma: *share doshta oilo* time *na* age? (is *share doshta* time or age?)

Raihan: age

Fahmida: no, time, time

Nazma:	good, *ar jodi koi share dosh bosor, toy ego* time *na* age? (and if we say *share dosh bosor*, then is it time or age?)
Nusrat:	age
Nazma:	well done, *tumi janlai kila?* (how did you know?) I think she knows, but do you want to tell me how you knew it was age and not time?
Nusrat:	because you said age in Bengali

Drawing their own number lines, children placed themselves, their siblings and friends in the correct places, helped by Nazma and Sarah. To practise the concepts of age and time, Nazma gave them phrases to translate between Bangla and English, such as 'Mohammed is seven and a half, and likes watching EastEnders at half past seven'. She called *bosor* and *ta* the 'magic words', and the children became quite proficient in using them. Children then created their own similar phrases, speaking both Bangla and English, and all using *share* for 'half' as well as the magic words for age and time. They showed facility in dealing with the concept of 'half' across the different domains of age and time, having made the connections in Bangla and translated the idea into English.

Developing metalinguistic skills

If you only use one language for learning, you will not necessarily notice how it operates. But as soon as you have another language to compare it with, you start to find similarities and differences. In English adjectives come before nouns, as in 'black cat', but in many languages – for instance in Spanish – it will be 'cat black' (*gato negro*). This difference draws attention to what kind of word 'cat' is, compared to 'black'. Bilingual children become aware that 'cat', 'dog' and 'mouse' belong to one category, whereas 'black', 'brown' or 'purple' are in another. They also realise that word order can be different. Meanwhile, in German or Bengali, verbs come at the end of a phrase instead of in the middle, and this highlights the concept of 'verb'.

Such knowledge about language, called metalinguistic knowledge, can be gained at a very young age, as shown by six-year-olds explaining how writing works in Chinese, Arabic or Spanish compared to English (Kenner, 2004a). Children can be encouraged to express and develop this knowledge as part of their learning at school. Viv Edwards, Frank Monaghan and John Knight (2000) found that pupils in South Wales who made bilingual multimedia storybooks began to generate hypotheses about word order and pronoun use in Welsh and English. Raymonde Sneddon (2009) gives examples of children making creative comparisons between grammatical structures in Turkish and

English when reading a dual-language book together. According to Vygotsky (1962), reflecting on different linguistic systems aids the development of children's thinking. The children we were working with were mostly stronger in English than Bangla, but we thought it very likely they would be aware of differences between their language systems and we were curious about the ideas they would generate if asked to make comparisons.

No 'the' in Bangla

We found children's bilingualism sharpened their knowledge about how language works. Jameela, Miqdad, Amal and Junel, seven-year-olds from School A, showed their ideas in a discussion with their class teacher, Owen. The children had translated the Lion and Mouse fable from Bangla into English, working from a version in transliterated Bangla by Jameela's nine-year-old sister Hanna (Figure 5).

Figure 5: Hanna's version of The Lion and the Mouse

By comparing their translation with Hanna's original version, Owen could see the English words did not map directly onto the Bengali ones. Sitting round a table with the group, he asked them to explain. The first issue that arose was about the definite article 'the', which is necessary in English but not used in Bangla.

Jameela:	(reads out) The lion is sleeping in the cave
Owen:	Where's the word 'the'? (noticing there are fewer words in Hanna's Bangla version, *shingho goomayse caveor bitre*)
Miqdad:	No 'the'!
Owen:	Why didn't you just say 'lion is sleeping'?
Amal:	Because there is 'the' in there but when you say it in English you add the 'the'

Amal meant that the word lion in Bangla could be taken to include the definite article, whereas if you were saying lion in English you would need to specify it.

She continued:

if a person was talking to another person and the person was saying a word, and said it without 'the', the other person would know because...

Here Amal explained that if two people were talking in Bangla, they would share an understanding that the definite article was not necessary. She was aware of this grammatical difference between English and Bangla and was able to express it to her teacher.

The children showed their understanding of word order in Bangla and English, and of differences in use of grammatical structure and prepositions, when they discussed how to translate the following phrase:

Tow oondure	*shinghor*	*loge*	*mattse*	(transliterated Bangla)
Then mouse	lion's	with	talking	(literal translation)
Then the mouse started talking to the lion				(the children's translation)

The children had no problem with immediately re-ordering the sentence as they translated it, since they were accustomed to the verb coming after the subject in English, whereas it would be at the end of the phrase in Bangla. So Junel began the translation process for this sentence by saying: 'the mouse told the lion', quickly rephrasing it as 'the mouse started to talk to the lion'. Miqdad agreed with 'started to talk' but pointed out the literal translation 'with the lion'. Jameela supported Junel's idea by emphasising 'started to talk to the lion', which sounds better in English. When Owen asked why the children had changed the word order and added 'started', they said 'it makes more sense'. Thus when children were encouraged to discuss differences between language structure in Bangla and English, they made their knowledge more explicit and developed their ideas.

Building cultural knowledge

Growing up with different cultural experiences increases opportunities for learning because you have access to a range of knowledge and expertise, from practical skills to abstract ideas. Learning at school can thus be enhanced by drawing on children's home and community knowledge as part of the curriculum. This approach can help children understand aspects of mainstream culture that are new to them, by making links with more familiar experiences. Marilyn Martin-Jones and Mukul Saxena (2003) discuss how a bilingual assistant in a Northwest England primary school helped children understand how weighing scales worked, by explaining in Panjabi and showing how the equipment related to the practice of measuring out flour in fistfuls when making chapattis. Panjabi was also used when storyreading, to 'anchor the world of the storybook' to home knowledge.

Children's writing can be stimulated by stories from their cultural background; Manjula Datta (2007) gives examples of work in London classrooms, from a Bangladeshi five-year-old writing a story based on the ghost world of his home culture, to young poetry writers inspired by Hindu mythology and Bollywood films. Children of second and third generation heritage have a considerable variety of cultural knowledge, both from mainstream culture and from their families and communities, due to their experience of living in 'simultaneous worlds' (Kenner, 2004b). When both worlds are relatively familiar, how can teachers help children make the most of these multicultural resources to benefit their learning?

Calculating with cousins

As the second or third generation in their families to live in the UK, the children in our project were growing up in a multicultural context. They had experiences and interests developed through English in mainstream school, but also felt closely involved with their Bangladeshi heritage – a culture partly their own yet partly unknown. Bilingual activities gave them the chance both to draw on the range of their cultural knowledge and to extend it.

For example, Bangladeshi culture is rooted in complex kinship relationships. There are eight possible categories of cousin, each with a different title (such as '*sasar goror bai*' for 'paternal uncle's son'). We made use of this as part of the bilingual word problem activities. The Year 6 children in School B were asked to fill in a chart by writing the names of their own cousins in the eight categories. These would be used as material for the word problems, to calculate how many cousins there were on their mother's side, or how many girl cousins they had in one particular category. We found children were aware of these kinship relationships but could not always remember the titles. By working on the task, they clarified and consolidated their understanding. They all managed to fill in their charts. Iqbal and Suraiya had cousins in all eight categories, Iqbal with 17 altogether and Suraiya with 33. The children tackled word problems such as 'All but seven cousins on your mother's side have been invited to a wedding, so how many will go?' and developed their own problems based on the chart.

Sharing faith stories

Children tend to relate strongly to stories that come from their home setting, and in the case of the Bangladeshi Muslim community in Tower Hamlets, these are often faith stories. Many have connections with stories from other faiths, so could be told and compared in class as part of literacy or religious education. However, teachers in mainstream schools rarely invite children to bring and share such material. When the Year 4 children were preparing their display on learning Bangla, referred to earlier, they talked about their faith classes and wanted to share faith stories with their teacher.

The children and their teacher Ella sat cross-legged on the floor to share stories. The importance of faith to the children became apparent as Maisha told a story about Prophet Muhammad. When Nayim told the story of Ibrahim, Ella recognised it as the Bible story about Abraham. The storytelling interactions had a different quality from religious education lessons we had observed in the school, even though those also covered a variety of faiths. On this occasion, the teacher physically positioned herself alongside the children, and invited them to share their knowledge from community classes. Her approach constructed a more equal relationship in which children were recognised as partners in learning. In this way she discovered they could tell rich and well-developed stories that were particularly significant to them.

Building learner identities

We all engage in a continual process of constructing our identities through everyday practices and relationships with other people. If different languages and cultures are part of your life, they will contribute to multiple aspects of your identity, all of which will be important to your sense of self. In contexts where the different aspects of your identity are recognised, you are likely to feel more at ease. Research by Angela Creese and colleagues in complementary schools (Creese *et al*, 2006) demonstrates that children can explore a range of identities in these settings because they are able to use their different languages for interaction and for learning. They show affiliation to their heritage language identities, and also develop multicultural identities, drawing on mainstream culture as well as the cultures of their families and communities. In addition, they are encouraged to construct confident learner identities, with their language knowledge contributing to their academic success.

If mainstream schools also give children the chance to use their linguistic and cultural knowledge, their learning can progress, as shown by Jim Cummins and colleagues (Cummins and Early, 2011) through students' production of 'identity texts' in educational settings around the world. We wanted to discover whether children of second and third generation heritage would feel differently about themselves as learners if they could work bilingually on tasks across the curriculum that related to the full range of their cultural experience.

Bangla as part of school

As they worked on the project activities, children became more self-assured about using Bangla and bringing to the fore aspects of their identities linked with home language. They also gained confidence about using Bangla in the presence of their teachers. We asked the Year 2 group in School A who worked on The Lion and the Mouse story how they felt about discussing their translation with their teacher Owen, and Jameela replied 'I thought we were going to be nervous but I wasn't'. The children went on to explain how working in a group had helped them feel more secure about learning in Bangla:

> And we were like working in teams. We know what it [Bangla] means but we're too shy. When you came the first time we were a little bit shy.

Teachers began to talk with the groups about how they used bilingual approaches, which gave children opportunities to express their views. The Year 2 group in School B working on maths problems about age and time were asked by their teacher Sarah what language they were thinking in while doing the calculation. They said Bangla, and she enquired why, which led to the following conversation:

Raihan:	because we like Bangla
Sarah:	brilliant, that's as good a reason as any, yes
Maryam:	because we learn about Bangla
Fahmida:	in school, we want teachers to learn Bangla
Sarah:	yes, I think I've learnt a few new words

The children's explanations covered their emotional attachment to Bangla, and their wish to develop the language. Fahmida went further, stating: 'we want teachers to learn Bangla'. This suggests a sense of entitlement to use the language in school, and perhaps the hope that teachers could enter into children's worlds. In her response, Sarah acknowledged that she too could be a learner by participating in bilingual activities.

Case study: How bilingual poetry can enhance children's learning
In most of the project activities, the children demonstrated all five aspects of bilingual learning: transferring concepts between languages; making meaning through translation; developing metalinguistic skills; building cultural knowledge; and building learner identities. To show how this happened, we describe one of the activities in detail: the Year 6 group in School B working on Bengali and English lullabies.

Bangladesh has a strong literary tradition and has produced a Nobel Laureate, Rabindranath Tagore, as well as other important poets such as Kobi Nazrul. Their writings for children are studied in Bengali complementary classes in London, together with a wealth of traditional stories and poetry. Cara, the Year 6 teacher from School B, was keen to use Bengali poetry for a bilingual literacy activity. Together we chose a *chora* (Bengali poem) called *ai ai chad mama* (come, come uncle moon), shown in Figure 6 overleaf. Most children had heard it sung at home as a lullaby. This poem contains complex metaphors that are an excellent resource for a classroom poetry lesson. Cara was immediately reminded of a lullaby in English from North America, Hush Little Baby, and decided to devise activities comparing the two poems.

We discovered that only one of our Year 6 group, Suraiya, could read the poem in Bengali script. So we transliterated the poem and translated it, as shown below, and gave the children all three versions to maximise their understanding.

Figure 6: Bengali poem 'Ai ai chad mama' (Come, come uncle moon)

Ai ai chad mama
Come come uncle moon

ai ai chad mama tip die ja
Come come uncle moon and touch the forehead
chader kopale chad tip die ja
Moon come and touch the forehead of the moon
dhan banle kuro debo
When the rice is made I will give you the husk
mach katle muro debo
When the fish is cut I will give you the head
kalo gaer dudh debo
I will give you the milk of the black cow
dudh khabar bati debo
I will give you the bowl for the milk
chader kopale chad tip die ja
Moon come and touch the forehead of the moon

The mother, holding the baby in her arms, appeals to the moon to come and touch the baby's forehead, which is likened to the moon in terms of beauty and luminance. 'As beautiful as the moon' is a common saying in Bengali. The phrase *tip die ja* refers to placing a black dot on a child's forehead, a cultural practice in rural areas of Bangladesh, designed to protect the child from the 'evil eye'. The further implication is that by touching the baby's forehead the moon will help send her to sleep. In return, the mother offers gifts. The husk of the rice is a popular treat in Bangladeshi villages, a fried snack made with leftovers from turning paddy into rice. The fish head and cow's milk are also delicacies.

To fully comprehend such a poem, you need to understand metaphors and cultural references. Children are faced with a similar task when studying English literature, and often find it difficult. The Bengali *chora* gave them the chance to work on their ideas bilingually and ask their parents for help. The Year 6 group understood the words literally and sensed that some kind of exchange was involved: 'it's about the moon. ... I would give you this if you do this for me'; 'give things back to you'. But they told their teacher 'it's a bit tricky', and when Cara asked if their parents could explain, they chorused 'definitely, yeah'. They realised they needed additional information about the language and the cultural content of the poem.

The children worked as a group to compose questions in Bangla for their parents, writing in transliteration since it was quicker and easier. They each took their questions home, together with the three versions of the *chora*. Suraiya interviewed her parents in Bangla, noted the answers in English and translated them back into Bangla (Figure 7). This shows she thought about the meanings twice over, through both languages. She asked her parents to sign the task, putting it on the same footing as homework in English. Nazrin asked her mother the questions in Bangla and wrote her answers in English. This too involved thinking about the meaning in both languages. Iqbal also wrote some answers in English, whereas Ziaul did not write any answers at home. All the children benefited by sharing their ideas in the group discussion at their next bilingual session (Kenner *et al*, 2008a).

Developing metalinguistic skills through transliteration

The children drew on their metalinguistic awareness as they wrote questions in transliterated Bangla for their parents, discussing how best to represent Bangla sounds using English letters. Even though most of them had never used transliteration before, they applied phonic strategies learned in primary school and took great care to record pronunciation as correctly as possible. A discussion on how to transliterate the Bangla word *khene* (why) showed this:

> How do you spell *khene*?
>
> Just sound it out and...
>
> (They sound out *khene, khene*, emphasising the guttural sound at the beginning, typical of Sylheti though not used in Standard Bengali)
>
> Just write *kene*, OK

Two of the children settled on this, recognising that the sound could not be represented precisely through English script, but the other two preferred *khene*.

Understanding metaphor through conceptual transfer and translation

When composing questions for their parents, children grappled with the metaphorical ideas in the poem. At first they interpreted the meaning literally. One child asked 'why is the moon going to do the jobs?' Another was concerned about the bowl for the milk being given away to the moon: 'how will they get the bowl back?' Their questions (translated into English here) included:

> How's the moon going to touch the baby on the forehead?
> How will you give food to the moon?
> How will the moon eat food?

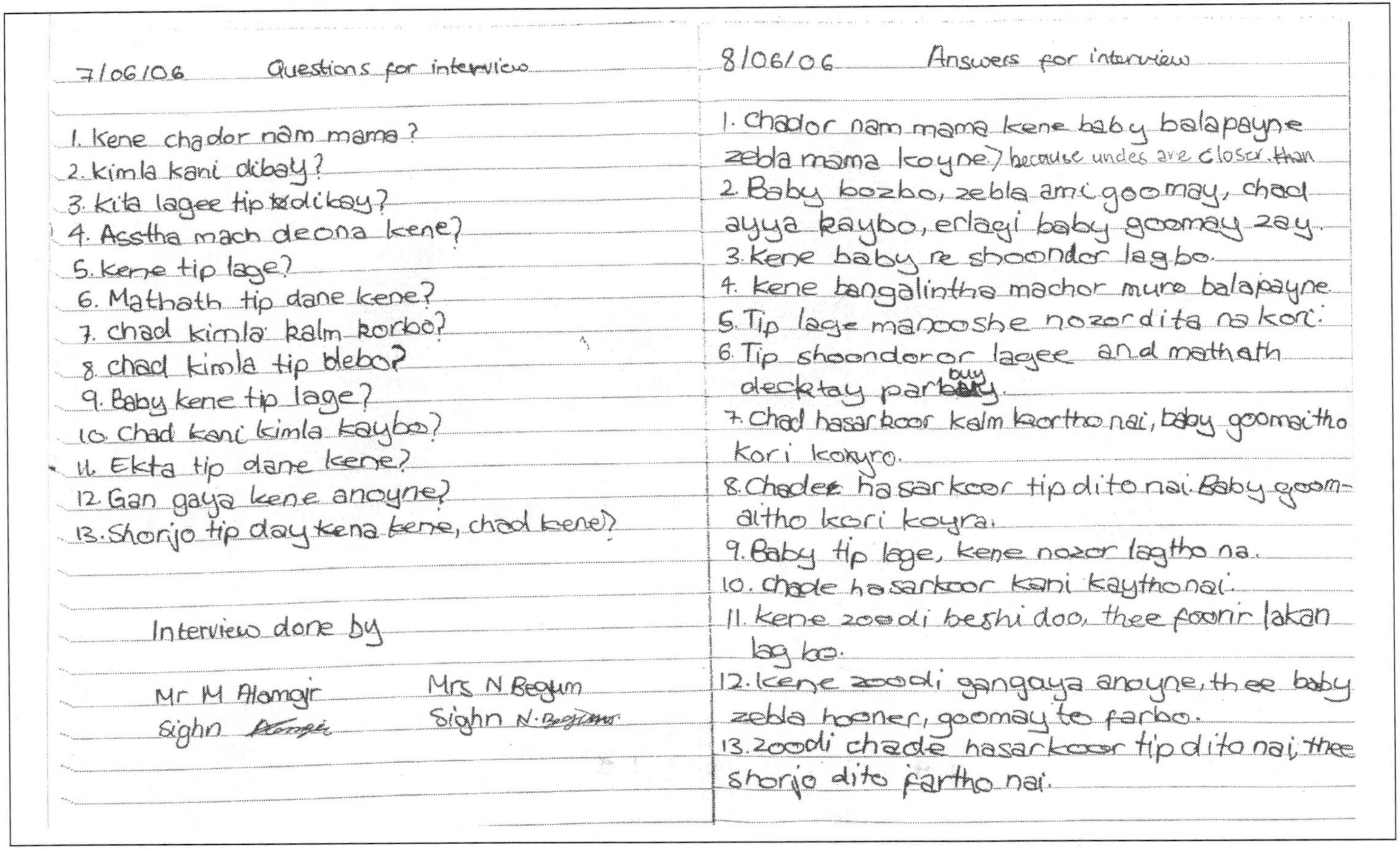

7/06/06   Questions for interview

1. kene chador näm mama?
2. kimla kani dibay?
3. kita lagee tip toditbay?
4. Asstha mach decna kene?
5. kene tip lage?
6. Mathoth tip dane kene?
7. chad kimla balm borboo?
8. chad kimla tip blebo?
9. Bay kene tip lage?
10. chad kani kimla kaybo?
11. Ekta tip dane kene?
12. Gan gaya kene anoyne?
13. Shonjo tip day kena tere, chad kene?

Interview done by

Mr M Alomgir   Mrs N Begum

Sighn kérépi   Sighn N. begzoor

8/06/06   Answers for interview

1. chador nam mama kene baby balapayne
zebla mama koyne) because undes are closer than
2. Baby bozbo, zebla ami goomay, chad
ayya kaybo, erlagi baby goomay zay.
3. kene baby re shoondor lagbo.
4. kene bangalintha machor mure balapayne
5. Tip lage manooshe nozordita na kor.
6. Tip shoonderor lagee and mathoth
decktay partay.
7. chad hasarkoor kalm korttho nai, baby goomaitho
kori koayro.
8. Chades ha sarkoor tip dito nai. Baby goom=
aitho kori koyra.
9. Baby tip lage, kene nozor lagtho na.
10. chade ho sarkoor tip kani kaytho nai.
11. kene zoodi beshi doo, thee koonr lakan
lag boo.
12. keene zoodi, gangaya anoyne, three baby
zebla hoener goomay to farbo.
13. zoodi chade hasarkoor tip dito nai, three
shonjo dito fartho nai.

Figure 7: Suraiya's questions for her parents

45

Suraiya discovered from talking in Bangla with her parents that metaphors were involved, and explained this to the others. When Nazrin asked 'is the moon really gonna come?', Suraiya answered 'no, cos the moon can't walk with feet'. Iqbal then asked '*chad kimla tip debo?*' (how will the moon give the spot?) and Suraiya replied 'he's not gonna really give it'. Starting to grasp the metaphor, Iqbal said 'faking it' and Suraiya underlined the idea with 'it's not the truth'. Nazrin, drawing on her discussion in Bangla with her mother, emphasised the poem's use as a lullaby: 'the mum is just trying to make the baby go to sleep, she's gonna hush him down'. Her mother had talked with her about the poetic aspects of the *chora*, and Nazrin had noted down 'the lady is using her imagination to calm her baby'. She had also written what she called an 'all in all statement' at the end of her mother's answers, which combined the practical and poetic effects: 'this story is just trying to get the baby to *khantona* (stop crying) and to make the reader think about the moon'. By providing both the Bengali word *khantona* and the English translation in brackets, Nazrin showed she was using both languages to explore the concepts involved in the *chora* fully. After the group discussion, which took place in Bangla and English, Iqbal and Ziaul also wrote that the mother is 'using her imagination'. By transferring concepts between languages and using translation to negotiate meaning, the group had reached collective agreement about the use of metaphor in the poem.

Exploring cultural content

The children engaged more fully with their Bangladeshi cultural heritage by studying the poem in school and mediating their learning through discussions with parents at home. At first they wondered why the moon was referred to as *mama* (maternal uncle). They were perplexed by the idea of offering a fish head as a gift. They were also fascinated by the idea of the *tip*. By pooling their existing knowledge, they worked out it was a 'black spot' placed on the forehead, but they had many other questions about it:

Why does the baby need the spot?
Why give the *tip* on the head instead of the hand or somewhere else?
Why is it going to give one black spot instead of lots?

The term *mama* (maternal uncle) is used to describe the moon because it expresses endearment and establishes a close relationship between mother and baby as the lullaby is sung. Relatives on the maternal side are regarded with particular affection in Bangladesh because they are seen less often, as most families live with the paternal relations. After talking with his mother about the poem, Iqbal wrote in his exercise book 'uncles are more closer'.

Ziaul expanded this point in the group discussion, stating *mama shob amrar thake amrar* (maternal uncle, we all have maternal uncle). Iqbal responded with 'close' and Ziaul emphasised the special feeling within a Bangladeshi family by using the Bangla word *daro.* Suraiya realised Cara would not know about kinship terms, and explained to her at the end of the session: 'the moon is called uncle moon, because in English uncles are any kind of uncle and in Bengali ... *mama* is the mum's brother, and they're more closer'.

Suraiya had asked her parents about the use of the fish head as a gift and written the answer:

> *asstha mach deona kene?*
> (Why don't you give the full fish?)
> *kene banglaintha machor muro balapayne*
> (Because Bengali people like the fish head)

When Iqbal looked puzzled, Suraiya expanded: 'the best part of the fish is the head, but the body part isn't cos it's just the normal fish, but the head is like crunchy and everything and it's got brain in it'. Iqbal's 'oh' showed his understanding, and he and Ziaul wrote in their exercise books 'head is the tasty bit in the body'. Later Ziaul confirmed his new understanding by explaining to Cara that the mother in the poem 'offers the moon some gifts so she can thank him for what he did – the head of the fish, some rice, a bowl for the milk'.

The questions about the *tip* (black spot) generated responses from several of the parents and some discussion amongst the children. Iqbal had initially written 'spot makes you more brainy', but Suraiya contested this: 'no, because ... it looks more like a beauty spot'. This was one of the answers her parents had given: 'the *tip* is for beauty'. She also understood from translating and writing her parents' other answer ('We need to touch the forehead so that people can't cast the evil eye') that the black spot was given to protect the baby, and shared this explanation with her classmates and Cara.

Cultural contrasts

Cultural aspects of the *chora* were highlighted when children compared it with the lullaby Hush Little Baby, which begins:

> Hush, little baby, don't say a word,
> Papa's gonna buy you a mockingbird.
> And if that mockingbird don't sing,
> Papa's gonna buy you a diamond ring.

The children recognised this poem from school culture and mainstream popular culture. They had learnt it in school at the age of five, and the rap singer Eminem had recently recorded a new version. They quickly began to find similarities with the *chora*, noting that 'it's about babies' and involved some form of persuasion because 'if you don't do something – don't cry – then you're gonna give something'. When asked for differences, they pointed out 'it's not talking about the moon' and 'it's gonna be the baby that gets them [ie the presents]'. Cara asked the group to use a Venn diagram, consisting of two overlapping circles, to compare the lullabies. They wrote down the similarities between the poems in the central overlapping part and the differences on either side, with points only arising in *Ai ai chad mama* on one side and Hush Little Baby on the other (see Figure 8).

One point was the type of gifts being offered. At first, when asked by Cara whether the gifts in the *chora* were good ones, the children thought 'not really'. Suraiya commented 'they're gonna waste out'. But when comparing the presents of food in the *chora* with the diamond ring and the looking glass offered in Hush Little Baby, they began to see the advantages of the Bangladeshi gifts: 'this is useful, this one it can break and stuff, it's breakable'. The concept of what is valued in different cultures thus came to the fore. Nazrin wrote on the *chora* side of the Venn diagram 'these gifts are important, because they're food' whereas 'Hush little baby's gifts are not for useful reasons'. When Cara returned at the end of their group discussion, and asked again whether the Bangladeshi gifts were good, some children said 'no' (perhaps equating the idea of 'good' in UK culture with 'expensive'), but Iqbal pointed out that 'if you were poor, you'd much rather have this stuff'.

The children also evaluated the effectiveness of the arguments in each lullaby to persuade the baby to go to sleep. They had an animated discussion about whether the mother in the *chora* was 'blackmailing' the moon because the gifts would only be given when her wishes were granted, and whether the Hush Little Baby singer was making 'excuses' for the anticipated failure of each gift. They were enthusiastic about comparing the lullabies, 'cos one's Bengali and one's English and that makes it different. Sometimes if it's Hush Little Baby and another English poem then you can't make the difference'. Cara commented that cultural variety had stimulated the children's learning, generating ideas that would not have arisen from studying poetry in English only.

Multiple identities

Cara explicitly encouraged the children to use Bangla when she introduced the *chora* work, saying 'you can speak Bangla and you should be speaking

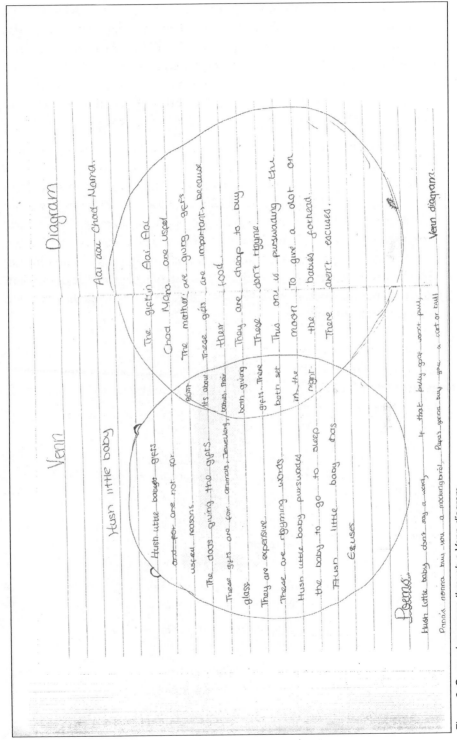

Figure 8: Comparing poems through a Venn diagram

Bangla – you can also write in Bangla or if you want to use a mix of both, it's up to you'. Left alone to work on the Venn diagram, children began to relax and speak Bangla into the microphone of the audiorecorder. One said 'I feel very very Bangla today'. As they drew their diagrams, they switched from singing the rap version of Hush Little Baby to the one they had learned in primary school and then to *Ai ai chad mama*, thus bringing together the different aspects of their identities from popular culture, school and home.

When the children shared their parents' answers, Cara again encouraged them to use Bangla. Iqbal was the most determined at the start, saying *Bangla maat* (speak in Bangla) and insisting everyone used the word *chora* instead of 'poem'. The group again began playing with language, speaking Bangla with an English accent and vice versa. Gradually they switched languages more freely and used Bangla as well as English for both informal talk and academic discussion. Finally Iqbal spoke Bangla when Cara returned and translated for her when they were reporting their findings. The children became more confident in their bilingual identities as the session progressed, and made the transition to using Bangla for learning.

Becoming writers in Bangla

The activity finished with the children writing their own poems in transliterated Bangla, with the help of bilingual teaching assistant Nazma. One of the poems appears below:

Fruits

grisho milee kaatol aam
we get mangoes and jackfruits in summer

shada jam, kalo jam
white berries, black berries

kalo angoor, shobuj angoor
black grapes, green grapes

holood ronger pakna kola
yellow-coloured ripe bananas

shobuj ronger kasa kola
green-coloured tender bananas

tenga boroy, mita boroy
sour berries, sweet berries

kaite lage bala
taste very sweet

This was the first time the children had ever written a poem in Bangla. The poem shows both rhythm and rhyme. The content combines fruits encountered through life in England and in Bangladesh. The children presented their writing to Cara with pride. It was a fitting conclusion to the poetry work, in which their conceptual and cultural understanding had advanced and their confidence as bilingual learners had increased markedly.

Whole-class lessons

Having investigated the potential for bilingual learning through small group activities, the teachers moved on to devise whole-class lessons with the help of Bangla-speaking teaching assistants. Cara and Nazma jointly planned and delivered a lesson for a Year 5 class, exploring similarities and differences between the Bengali and English lullabies discussed above. All the children in the class responded positively, whether they were monolingual English-speaking or spoke other languages such as Somali, or were part of the majority British Bangladeshi group.

By working with the transliterated and translated versions of the *chora*, the non-Bangla speakers could read out the poem and talk about it. Together the children discussed the content of the lullaby, fascinated by ideas such as protecting the baby from the evil eye (which they compared to similar practices in other cultures) and the concept of calling the moon 'uncle'. The Venn diagram activity again stimulated a variety of comparisons between the two lullabies.

Nazma and Cara taught in partnership, with Nazma encouraging the children of Bangladeshi origin to use both languages by modelling structures such as 'Why does the poet use the word...?' and 'What does ... mean?' in Bangla as well as English. Children showed sensitivity about code-switching so that their non-Bangla speaking peers could also understand. The children new to Bangla asked questions about the meaning of Bangla words and how the language worked. A Somali-speaking child said 'when I spoke a little bit of it from that Bengali writing ... I felt that I need to learn more of it' and suggested also writing in Somali. A monolingual child commented: 'When I used Bengali it made me feel different because it was other people's language – I didn't know it at first – when I started to try it, it made me feel a bit different'. She confirmed this was a positive feeling. So rather than excluding non-Bangla speakers, the bilingual session promoted inclusion. Children were finally able to engage with Bangla, a language they heard spoken in the playground but had little chance to learn. The work began to create a multilingual ethos in the class, encouraging children to mention their knowledge of other languages too.

Similar findings arose from other whole-class lessons. Owen taught a lesson in which a Year 3 class compared three versions of The Hare and Tortoise fable prepared with the help of Bengali teacher Rakib. They looked at the story in Bengali script, transliterated Bangla and English translation. Children used their existing knowledge of the story to predict meanings in Bangla. They compared language structures and explored meanings that did not exactly translate. In one case they sought different possible translations for the Bangla phrase *khorgushti gobir goomey goomaya porilo* (literally 'the hare slept sleeping'). In Bangla, repetition of the verb is used for emphasis. The children's ideas included 'slept so long' and 'slept and slept'. Fatima, the bilingual teaching assistant co-presenting the lesson, suggested 'the hare fell into a deep sleep'.

Meanwhile, Ella devised a numeracy lesson in which logic problems were given in transliterated Bangla as well as in English. Working bilingually in small groups, children enthusiastically solved problems such as how a small boat could be used to transport different combinations of passengers across a river. The teachers' experience indicates that bilingual work can build positive relationships within the whole class as children explore the conceptually challenging terrain of multilingual learning.

Bilingual strategies for mainstream school

The research highlighted strategies that educators can use to promote bilingual learning as part of the curriculum. These strategies can be deployed even if teachers are monolingual themselves, and in classes where the children have a variety of home languages. Since our research was with children from second and third generation bilingual backgrounds, it is particularly important to offer additional support for their home languages as well as English. Below we explain the strategies of transliteration, collaborating with families, providing bilingual resources, and presenting key vocabulary and language structures bilingually.

Using transliteration

Transliteration opens the door to bilingual learning. Children are often at a beginner level in reading and writing in their mother tongue, since even those who attend complementary classes only do so for a few hours a week. However, every child who speaks a language can write it in transliteration, using English letters. Then non-Bangla speaking teachers and children can also read out words and phrases and discuss meanings together with Bangla speakers.

We do not see transliteration as a substitute for learning the correct script. Rather, we find transliteration to be a bridge to learning. It operates in the following ways:

- as a communicative bridge, enabling children to share ideas with parents and teachers
- as a conceptual bridge, promoting reflection on meaning and language structure
- as a bridge to Bengali script, because children can study the sounds and work out how to represent them using Bengali letters
- as a bridge to new learner identities, building children's confidence as bilingual writers

Our team has explored these issues in detail elsewhere (Al-Azami *et al*, 2010). Here we give a few examples from the work done by the Year 2 children at School A on the Lion and Mouse story.

Transliteration as a communicative bridge

The Year 2 teacher Owen adopted a 'Story Sharing' approach, sending home a picture-only version of the Lion and Mouse story, with a letter asking parents to write their own captions together with their children. The title of the story was transliterated into both Standard Bengali and Sylheti, to encourage parents and children to write in transliteration if they wished:

> *shingho ow idhur* ('the lion and the mouse' in Standard Bengali, transliterated)
> *shingho ow oondur* ('the lion and the mouse' in Sylheti, transliterated)

To facilitate the discussion with parents, Owen asked the four children to prepare questions in transliterated Bangla. He explained that they should 'use Bangla, but use English letters to sound it out'. Responses came back in a range of forms, written by parents or children, in Bengali script or transliterated Sylheti, some including English words as well. The answers demonstrated how the transliterated questions had stimulated intergenerational communication around the story. For example, one of Miqdad's questions was:

> *Shingho oondur re cay no cene?*
> (Why does the lion not eat the mouse?)

The answer from his father in Bengali script (translated below) was fairly complex, giving an overview of the story:

> When the lion was caught in a hunter's net, the mouse cut the net and helped the lion get out. And that's why the lion didn't eat the mouse.

Father and son would have discussed this in spoken Bangla and Miqdad's father gave him some access to the written answer by putting the key words *shingho* (lion) and *oondur* (mouse) in transliteration. Communication was also fostered between the children and their teacher. When Owen saw the Lion and Mouse story in transliterated Bangla and English, he was able to discuss with the children some of the differences between the two languages, as we described in the example of 'the' not being used in Bangla.

A conceptual bridge

Transliteration gave children the chance to reflect on words they had written down, encouraging them to think more deeply about language structure, as in their discussion with Owen, and about meanings. As they collectively composed their own version of Lion and Mouse in Bangla, they encountered the word 'caught' at two different points in the story. In the phrase 'the lion caught the mouse', the children knew *dorse* was the correct Bangla word. But when it came to the lion being caught in a net, they realised *dorse* was not appropriate. 'Caught' covered both meanings in English, whereas different words would be used in Bangla. The meaning of 'caught' in the second phrase would be 'trapped', and is passive rather than active. So instead of taking the English word 'caught' for granted, the children had to think about its different possible meanings in different circumstances. By exploring alternative translations, they enriched their understanding of the words involved and of the events in the story.

When transliterating, children had to consider sound-symbol relationships more deeply than when writing only in English. They slowly sounded out the Bangla words and talked together about how best to represent them, transferring their phonetic knowledge from English but recognising there was more than one possible answer. We can see their individual decisions in a phrase that each transliterated slightly differently, trying to capture the subtle differences between Bangla and English sounds:

Jameela	thara khoson 'Na!'
Junel	Tara coisoin 'NA!'
Miqdad	tara khoisoin 'NA'!
Amal	tara koyson 'Na'!

(English translation: they said 'NO!')

A bridge to Bengali script

Children can also work in the other direction, from transliteration to the script. A good example came when Tasnim, one of the Year 4 children at

School A, was trying to write a story in Bangla. She found it very difficult to write in Bengali script, so she used transliteration first. Once she could see the words written down, she sounded them out and worked out which letters to use in Bengali script. Although she initially predicted that she would only be able to write one or two words in the script, she actually managed twelve words quite quickly because this approach proved so fruitful.

A bridge to new learner identities

Transliteration gave children the chance to be authors, and they proved to be motivated and enthusiastic writers in Bangla. They rapidly grasped the concept of transliteration and its potential. Junel said 'It's exciting – it's something that I learned' and Miqdad said 'Cool. Different. We never done it before'. Collectively the children said, 'It's easy – we just think and we know how to write it'. They realised they could express their thoughts in Bangla through transliteration 'because then we know what it says. If we write in Bangla [ie Bengali script] we don't know what it says but if we write like this...' Transliteration is thus liberating and empowering for bilingual children who would otherwise be limited to expressing themselves in English in their writing.

Collaborating with families

The research showed how parents and other family members are key partners in learning. They provide important linguistic and cultural input, especially for children less confident in mother tongue. They can be invited to lead activities or assist in the classroom, as Nusrat's grandmother did when she helped the Year 2 children discuss *Snow White* and write in Bengali script. Questions can be devised by children, written in transliteration if necessary, and taken home, as we saw with the questions for parents on the Bengali lullaby. And other tasks such as the Story Sharing activity about the Lion and the Mouse fable can be undertaken together with family members at home.

Providing bilingual resources

With the help of community language teachers and bilingual assistants, or parents and families, teachers can produce resources for bilingual work that support learning in both English and mother tongue. Examples from our project include The Hare and Tortoise storybooks in parallel versions: English, Bengali script and transliterated Bangla. This gave children maximum support for understanding the content, and enabled them to compare how meanings were expressed in different languages.

Similarly useful was a bilingual dictionary produced locally in Tower Hamlets, using the same principle (providing each word in English, Bengali script, transliterated Standard Bengali and transliterated Sylheti). Another initiative was to make cards containing logic problems for mathematics in English on one side, translated and transliterated into Bangla on the other side. Children were encouraged to work out what the problem was about in one language, check their understanding by reading the other side of the card, and finally use both languages to discuss the solution. Materials were also created to support numeracy, such as '100 squares' in Bengali numerals as a parallel resource to English ones.

Presenting key vocabulary and language structures bilingually

It is good practice in the teaching of English as an Additional Language to check understanding of key vocabulary before an activity and help children rehearse language structures that enhance thinking skills, such as 'I wonder what will happen if we...?' or 'It might happen because....' (NALDIC, 2012b). Our findings showed that if bilingual learning is to be put into practice in schools, children also need to discuss vocabulary and modelling of structures in mother tongue. The skills of bilingual assistants can be used through partnership teaching, as in the example of Cara and Nazma working collaboratively to introduce the bilingual poetry activity, rehearsing typical phrases in both Bangla and English that facilitated discussion of literary meanings. For the Hare and Tortoise story, bilingual assistant Fatima worked with Owen to present transliterated Bangla words on the interactive whiteboard. Children could drag the words across the whiteboard to match them up with their English equivalents. Children can also research key vocabulary and language structures with parents and grandparents before the lesson.

Children in our project used Bangla appropriately for groupwork in whole-class bilingual lessons. Teachers who did not speak Bangla could see that the children were involved in their work and distinguish if talk went off-task. Children were sensitive to the needs of others and would not speak Bangla if grouped with those who did not understand it. One of the teachers suggested that pairings and groupings could be rotated in different lessons so that children were given the opportunity whenever possible to work with Talk Partners or groups who shared their mother tongue.

The need for academic language in mother tongue

It became clear during the research that children were fluent in everyday talk but lacked the language they needed for academic learning in Bangla. For example, the Year 2 children in School B did not know how to say 'four and a half years old' or 'half past four' in Bangla until Nazma introduced these terms when working on concepts of age and time. Children were aware of this lack and wanted to learn academic language in Bangla.

When the Year 6 group reflected on the experience of solving logic problems bilingually, they all said it was important to be able to do maths in Bangla as well as English. Suraiya and Nazrin said 'you understand more' and Ziaul said 'we can learn in two different ways', suggesting that bilingual learning helped them to grasp concepts and introduced a range of new ideas. However, Iqbal pointed out that 'in Bangla we don't know that much ... like the numbers, not that much about numbers and the signs and everything' and Suraiya agreed: 'the numbers and operations we want to find out more, how to say it and everything'.

There was a striking contrast between the children's developing knowledge of English at school and their lack of opportunity to develop Bangla for academic purposes. As Iqbal went on to say: 'we know lots of stuff about English but not that much about Bangla yet'. Children had a strong emotional identification with Bangla as the language of their home and family, but English dominated as soon as they entered mainstream schooling. Suraiya's final comment was particularly poignant: 'Bangla is our mother tongue but we don't know much about it.'

Even though the children were growing up in Tower Hamlets, known as 'Banglatown', everyday social interactions were often conducted partly in English and were insufficient to develop full knowledge of Bangla, particularly of an academic repertoire. Our findings are similar to those of Eilers and colleagues in research with second and third generation Spanish-speaking children in Miami (Eilers *et al*, 2006). Like their Tower Hamlets counterparts, these children live in a community where their mother tongue is regularly used in the business and social infrastructure but they are losing their Spanish competence unless they are also schooled in Spanish. This highlights the crucial role that can be played by mainstream schools in encouraging bilingual learning as part of the curriculum and in making links with parents to support academic work in mother tongue at home.

Teachers' views on bilingual learning

Teachers were impressed by the children's response to bilingual learning. Cara observed that the project had meant 'seeing the children in a different way', since they felt empowered when demonstrating their knowledge in

Bangla. Owen said 'It's their script ... it's their language ... when they see it they're very excited'. Bilingual learning turned out to be relevant to each child in particular ways. Children with apparent learning difficulties in English were often more confident in mother tongue, such as the girl who 'woke up' on hearing Bangla in a whole-class bilingual lesson, and volunteered an accurate Bangla translation of the moral of the Hare and Tortoise story: 'slow and steady wins the race'. Children with surface fluency in English but un-confident in academic language understood concepts more easily when they could use both languages. Children already identified as academically suc-cessful were revealed to have a particularly strong background in Bangla as well as being highly competent in English. When they could work in both languages, their learning was further enhanced. So bilingual learning has the potential to foster educational achievement for a wide range of children with differing levels of knowledge of mother tongue and English.

Through direct experience, teachers gained a fuller understanding of how bilingual learning worked, as encapsulated in Owen's comment: 'Any child who has more than one language, it makes them more confident and they can apply those skills to another language'. Also, by treating children as bi-lingual rather than monolingual learners, the teachers engaged more fully with important areas of cultural experience. As Sarah put it, the children 'have so much life outside of school – school is only part of their life'. Teachers now understood their pupils' identities more fully. Ella said of Bangla 'It's part of who they are'.

The project showed that children could engage with tasks bilingually even when English was their stronger language. By using the full repertoire of their linguistic and cultural knowledge they developed deeper understand-ing of concepts, activated metalinguistic skills and generated new ideas that enriched their learning. However, children were in danger of losing these advantages unless they had sufficient support to develop their mother tongue. Accordingly, one of the schools in our project chose to implement the teach-ing of Bengali as part of the primary languages curriculum, seeing it as bene-ficial for both the children of Bangladeshi origin and for their peers who could learn it as the language used in the community around them.

However, we realised there was a crucial step that had yet to be taken. Main-stream teachers were now aware that children's learning in complementary school was important, but none had yet visited a complementary class to see this learning in action. Consequently, the next stage of our research was dedicated to making direct links between mainstream and community edu-cators, and this is described in the second part of the book.

Ideas for promoting bilingual learning

- Children new to English will find it easier to generate ideas by speaking or writing in mother tongue, because they have vocabulary and language structures to support their thinking. They can then transfer these ideas to English. If children are accustomed to communicating bilingually, even if English is their stronger language, they will develop a greater range of ideas and enhance their thinking by using both languages. So it is important to give children opportunities to write ideas down in mother tongue as well as English, to work with bilingual talk partners in class and to discuss academic work bilingually with parents at home.

- If children are not familiar with their mother tongue script, they can express their ideas via transliteration into Roman script. This practice may be new to children so they will require examples, and these can be given with the help of bilingual assistants or parents. Teachers can encourage children to explore the best way to represent sounds from their language. If the child's mother tongue is written in Roman script, they can work out which symbols have different sounds from the English ones.

- You can start to bring children's multilingual identities into learning through activities that connect with their home and community lives. Children can research topics in different languages by writing questions for parents and grandparents and bringing answers back to share in class. The internet offers news and information in many languages. Curriculum topics can be enriched by children and families contributing poems, stories, historical information, maps, newspapers and web printouts in a range of different languages. Children can translate this material to make multilingual posters and presentations.

- Parents and other family members can be invited into school to support children's bilingual speaking and writing. Stories in first language can be shared with the class and parallel stories found in other languages and English. Parents and other bilingual adults can help investigate metaphors and similes through translation. Family members can be interviewed about life and work in the UK and elsewhere, with children as translators. Children can make short bilingual films or slide shows to present findings from these interviews.

- To fully exploit the advantages of bilingual learning, children need academic vocabulary in first language as well as English. Talk at home often uses non-academic terms, so children may need to research key vocabulary with the help of parents, bilingual dictionaries or internet translation software. A number of local authority ethnic minority achievement teams provide subject vocabulary lists in many languages (NALDIC, 2012a). Children can build up a multilingual class dictionary throughout the year. Bilingual adults can model key phrases in different languages to support children's discussions. For example, if children are classifying types of leaves in science, useful phrases to translate could include 'these leaves have different kinds of...' or 'these leaves are similar because they both have...'

- Bilingual learning can be supported through the languages curriculum. If one of the languages taught in school is the mother tongue of some of the pupils, this will aid their academic language development and offer all children benefits such as metalinguistic awareness and new cultural knowledge.

- Performing in different languages for a school event positively supports the development of children's multilingual identities. Children can work on this material as a resource for learning in class, investigating meanings and examining language structures to promote metalinguistic awareness.

3

Sharing Strategies

'Now that's what I call good practice!'

So said a primary school teacher after he had watched a videorecording of a grandmother teaching Bengali and Arabic to a small class of children in a home setting in East London. He was impressed by the strategies she used to support children aged from five to nine as they worked independently on reading or writing tasks at their own level. At the same time she managed to engage the attention of two active toddlers who were in the room by encouraging them to look at alphabet books and join in reciting Bengali poetry.

Immediately before seeing the video, this primary teacher had declared that complementary classes were occupying time in children's lives which could be more productively used. He was concerned that Bengali classes would be taught through traditional methods to which he thought children would respond negatively. He believed that many children growing up in Bangladeshi-origin families would derive more benefit from learning about the English side of life in London, for example by visiting nearby attractions such as Tower Bridge. Yet the video extract, which he saw and discussed as part of a seminar on bilingual learning, led him to appreciate the expertise of complementary teachers and recognise the importance of such language and literacy classes for children's education.

What counts as good practice in teaching? If they haven't ever visited complementary school classes, mainstream teachers may surmise that children there are being taught through 'chalk and talk' methods, which they assume to be repetitive and alienating. However, the reality is likely to be rather different and far more complex, as we can see from the skilful work of Nusrat's grandmother described above. Complementary teachers are faced with the challenge of devising approaches that meet the needs of mixed-age, multi-level classes of children growing up in changing linguistic and cultural contexts. The teachers respond creatively to this challenge, fuelled by a deep commitment to their pupils as individuals and as members of a learning community. Mainstream teachers have much to learn from the work of their complementary colleagues, and the combination of strategies from both contexts offers additional advantages.

In this chapter we first consider why complementary teachers' knowledge has been 'doubly devalued' by the mainstream education system. Although international research highlights the importance of home and community learning, the approaches used in this informal sector tend to go unacknowledged or unappreciated. The lack of recognition is exacerbated for teachers of community languages, since their area of expertise is considered irrelevant compared to children's study of dominant languages. We explain how this deficit view of work taking place in complementary schools is challenged by recent research studies, which reveal the wide range of teaching and learning strategies being developed there.

We then discuss our teacher partnership project involving mainstream and complementary teachers in East London. Our findings demonstrate that the work of complementary teachers should be 'doubly valued', because they use innovative community-based approaches and bilingual learning strategies that relate well to children's linguistic and cultural backgrounds. Partnership teaching creates mutual respect for each other's expertise, so that the knowledge exchanged by complementary and mainstream teachers is equally valued on both sides. As a result, partners can co-construct lessons by interweaving strategies to enhance their students' learning.

Home and community learning

From a socio-cultural perspective, education begins at home and continues in out-of-school settings, alongside children's experiences in mainstream school. A socio-cultural theory of learning (Vygotsky, 1978; Gregory *et al*, 2004) explains how children construct concepts through interaction with others, as they gradually become fully participant members of their communities. Children often play an active role in stimulating learning exchanges at home, as noted by Barbara Rogoff (2003) in ethnographic studies with families of US and Mayan backgrounds. As children undertook tasks with the help of their carers, Rogoff found they worked jointly in a relationship that she called 'guided participation'. Research in the UK by Eve Gregory (2001) and Charmian

Kenner (2005) on siblings learning together, and by Dinah Volk and Martha De Acosta in the US (2001), demonstrated that roles shift as older and younger children contribute to each other's learning. Gregory (2001) describes this interactive process as 'synergy'. Two-way learning happens as a younger parti-cipant actively questions an older one, leading them both to explore ideas further. Also, each participant may have different kinds of knowledge that come to the fore at certain points in the interaction. The latter situation is often the case when families migrate, because children develop the new lan-guage more quickly than their parents and may take the lead in activities re-quiring that language (Kenner, 2005). Particularly when children are learning with grandparents, older and younger generations exchange cultural and linguistic experiences from their country of origin and the new country res-pectively (Kenner *et al*, 2007; Gregory *et al*, 2007).

The flexibility of roles and interactive strategies that characterise home learn-ing can also be found in other out-of-school settings such as community-based classes. Teacher-student relationships may be more informal, and learning approaches used may vary depending on the expertise and needs of both teacher and learner, especially if the participants include adults and children from migration backgrounds. Examples come from a range of settings, from a homework club in a community centre in the US researched by Stacey Lee and Margaret Hawkins (2008), to a community art gallery in London where educators work with young people, studied by Paul Dash (2010). Later in this chapter, we discuss similar examples from research in complementary schools.

Teachers in home settings, such as siblings and grandparents, have an emo-tional and practical investment in the success of their learners. The child is expected to do well for their own sake, but also for the benefit of the family as a whole. This is particularly the case when a family has moved to a new country to improve their economic circumstances via the educational advancement of their children. Family members work collectively to support children's learning of the new language, whilst often trying to develop their mother tongue at the same time. Charmian Kenner's research with bilingual families in London (Kenner, 2005) shows how they operate as 'literacy eco-systems', in which adults and children pool their resources to achieve this dual aim. On a wider level, strong collective ties tend to be forged within a migration community making their way in a new environment and simul-taneously working to maintain their linguistic and cultural heritage. In such contexts, success for the child on both counts means progress for the com-munity. As we see shortly, complementary teachers aim for both children's individual achievement and that of the group, orienting their students to take responsibility not only for their own learning but also for that of their peers.

Although children tend to learn very effectively in home and community settings, many mainstream educators are unaware of this. Maria José Botelho and fellow educators in Canada (Botelho *et al*, 2009:250) urge teachers to 'expand our notion of where learning happens' by 'making sure that we as well as families are crossing the bridge between home/community and school'. They set up a summer institute programme which included literacy sessions held in a local mosque, and involved teachers from the mosque community and parent volunteers. US researchers and teacher educators Susi Long and Dinah Volk also encouraged teachers to visit community learning contexts and found such visits expanded their understanding (2009). Unfortunately such initiatives remain rare, and as Sonia Nieto and Patti Bode (2008) have argued, the power of dominant educational structures leaves little space for valuing learning that takes place outside the mainstream.

Teaching community languages: a job worth doing?

An additional difficulty for educators working in complementary schools is that policymakers regard the teaching of community languages as un-important. A major government report in the UK, the Swann Report (DES, 1985), stated that the government should not fund the teaching of com-munity languages but that this work should be the responsibility of com-munities themselves. The unspoken assumption was that such languages were of little value to mainstream society, and the complementary sector has been marginalised ever since. The Labour government of 2005-10 began to discover the benefits of complementary schools for children's learning, and funded the Our Languages project to link mainstream and complementary schools in 2008 and 2009 (Our Languages, 2012). They also awarded a grant to the National Resource Centre for Supplementary Education. This funding was short-term, however, and there was none for the basic needs of hard-pressed complementary schools across the UK.

In other English-dominant countries, community languages (also known as minority languages or heritage languages) have been similarly sidelined. Bilingual schooling within mainstream education in the US has come under attack from the 'English-only' movement (Crawford, 2000). Although some bilingual programmes still exist, heritage languages are often only used as a vehicle for transition to English, according to Nancy Hornberger and Shuhan Wang (2008:12). The result is, as Jim Cummins comments, 'massive attrition of students' heritage language competence over the course of schooling' (Cummins, 2005:585).

In Australia, although there are some excellent initiatives to include community languages in mainstream teaching, community languages still tend to be seen as marginal and there is a struggle to make them 'proper objects for policy attention', as Joe Lo Bianco (2008:67) notes. This view applies particularly to indigenous languages, in comparison to 'elite' languages used for international trade. Māori and Pasifika peoples in New Zealand continually campaign to receive equal consideration for their languages in education, despite the success of bilingual schooling projects in Māori or Samoan, as documented by Patisepa Tuafuti and John McCaffery (2005). Even in Canada, where heritage language education has shown good outcomes, aboriginal languages have only recently received funding, and Patricia Duff (2008) points out that many heritage language communities still struggle to run after-school or weekend classes with minimal resources.

Teachers in complementary schools are therefore subject to a dual discrimination, since they teach undervalued languages in undervalued educational settings. In the next section, we discuss what these 'doubly devalued' practitioners are actually accomplishing in terms of teaching and learning, according to recent research.

Teaching and learning in complementary schools

Practitioners in UK complementary schools face challenging conditions. Most work in borrowed spaces belonging to or used by others, from rooms in church halls or community centres to mainstream classrooms. Classes are often mixed-age, multi-level, or both. Practitioners have to make their own resources since some have textbooks from home countries but most have none, and access to ICT is rare. Some teachers are qualified in their home countries, some also work in the mainstream and others are dedicated volunteers from the community. And complementary teachers are poorly paid or not paid at all. This information comes from ethnographic research such as that of Eve Gregory and Ann Williams (2000), Kathy Hall and colleagues (2002), and Peter Martin and co-researchers (2007), and survey research by Tözün Issa and Claudette Williams (2009).

Despite or perhaps because of these conditions, teachers are keen to take up the rare possibilities for professional development. Those undertaking one of the few teacher education courses for community languages in the UK, organised at Goldsmiths, University of London by Jim Anderson (2008), identified the usefulness of resource development, planning, differentiation, inter-cultural and cross-curricular dimensions, and creative activities. Recent research by Jim Anderson and Yu-Chiao Chung (2011) showed complementary teachers quickly integrating arts-based creativity into their work when supported to do so.

A similar desire for training was found by Ping Liu (2006), researching with community-based Chinese teachers in Southern California. In Australia, complementary teachers took up opportunities offered by universities in response to the lobby group Community Languages Australia, whilst action research projects with Polish, Russian and Vietnamese teachers helped them incorporate new technologies and strategies for literacy learning (Clyne and Fernandez, 2008).

It would obviously be of great advantage if complementary teachers had better access to training and properly-resourced classrooms. However, it is remarkable how resilient and creative they are under difficult circumstances. The research we discuss below shows how their work is often underpinned by the strong teacher-student relationship and communal approach characteristic of informal learning settings. They have to invent, adapt and negotiate strategies to meet their learners' needs, including bilingual approaches that take into account the complex linguistic backgrounds of children who have grown up with English as their dominant language.

Complementary teachers tend to have close and supportive relationships with their students, because they are personally involved with their linguistic and cultural communities and have good links with parents, as described by Olga Barradas and Yangguang Chen (2008) in the UK and Anh Tran (2008) in the US. Hsu-Pai Wu and colleagues (2011) found that a group of Chinese heritage language teachers in the US saw their school as a community where participants should take care of each other and develop a sense of belonging. Hall *et al* (2002), studying complementary schools in England and Norway, identified a 'sense of solidarity' between teachers, children and parents that led students to talk of 'our school'. Teachers were 'authoritative but not authoritarian and relations between them and their students were friendly, sensitive and cheerful' (*ibid*:413). Teachers in the London Complementary Schools research project (Issa and Williams, 2009) showed dedication to their students; a typical comment was that 'you become their friend as well as their teacher'. In some cases, students develop more playful learner identities than in mainstream classrooms, as observed in Chinese schools in London by Becky Francis and co-researchers (2010).

The ethos of complementary schools is rather different from the individualistic competitive testing discourse that now characterises many mainstream educational systems. Parents and teachers are jointly committed to students' success as individuals who are members of a community with shared cultural as well as academic goals. Staff at complementary schools teach to their students' strengths (Hall *et al*, 2002) and help them develop confident learner identities (Creese *et al*, 2006). With such support, children can tackle language and literacy tasks, including activities required for community participation that present a considerable learning challenge. Examples come from a new study of four out-of-school faith settings in London (Gregory *et al*, forthcoming), where students practise and publicly perform lengthy and complex recitations, songs or dances.

To manage large or multi-level classes, complementary teachers often organise children into smaller groups and encourage independent learning. Andrey Rosowsky (2006:538) found that older or more advanced students 'facilitate and guide the learning' of other children in mosque classes in northern England, by acting as mentors or assistants to the teacher. Children may be given tasks to carry out independently whilst the teacher circulates to provide individual attention, as we noted in our bilingual learning research project (Kenner *et al*, 2008b). Hall *et al* (2002) also found that students received plenty of individual attention, and observed high levels of pupil-teacher interaction, teacher questioning, and some pupil-initiated questions.

Teachers in complementary schools find themselves exploring a range of strategies to meet the needs of students accustomed to mainstream education. In the UK, many also work as teaching assistants or teachers in mainstream schools, and can draw on this experience. For example, Jean Conteh and Shila Begum (2008) report on a Saturday school in Bradford where National Curriculum topics are taught through Punjabi and Bengali by primary teachers who are bilingual. If complementary teachers are drawing on training from their home country, they soon find students have different expectations. Teachers interviewed by Issa and Williams (2009:118) in London recognised that 'Children here are different. They need a number of approaches, not just one'.

Teachers in Chinese schools in Montreal (Curdt-Christiansen, 2006) continued with some traditional methodologies such as recitation of text, since this helped students internalise new words and phrases to use later in their own writing. However, the teachers also used questioning in a playful way to encourage imaginative thinking about the text. Meanwhile, teachers of

Chinese in the US with no previous training decided to share authority and co-construct learning with their students, and to create a 'joyful learning environment' (Wu *et al*, 2011:55) by introducing games. Similarly, Efstathia Pantazi (2010) describes how Greek teachers in London began to use communicative approaches involving visual stimuli, music and drama to engage their students.

Many children in complementary classes have little knowledge of their community language, especially if they are from second or third generation backgrounds. Teachers therefore develop bilingual strategies to assist their learning. Rather than using a 'target language only' approach, teacher and students switch between the dominant language and the community language to clarify meaning and build new understanding. Adrian Blackledge and Angela Creese (2010) call this approach 'flexible bilingualism'. Issa and Williams (2009) found that bilingual learning is a feature of complementary schools across London, and Pantazi (2010) also noted that teachers used 'bilingual reflection' judiciously, encouraging children to explore the Greek roots of words in English to link their knowledge of both languages.

Research findings therefore demonstrate that complementary teachers are strongly committed to their students and willing to explore strategies that meet the needs of their class. A recent survey for the UK government by Uvanney Maylor *et al* (2010) found complementary schools had a high level of parent and student satisfaction and made a notable contribution to pupils' overall educational achievement.

Research also shows that complementary teachers are seeking opportunities to link with the mainstream. Pantazi (2010) found Greek teachers want such engagement. The headteacher of a Turkish school in London interviewed by Issa and Williams (2009:48) commented 'we need to work very closely with mainstream and train our teachers but there is no coherent strategy to facilitate this'. Issa and Williams point to an obvious potential for local education authorities to establish complementary school forums for training and some in the UK have already done so, although their work is now constrained by financial cuts in the public sector. Through the Our Languages project, a number of UK mainstream schools offered training to the complementary sector from 2009 to 2010, demonstrating how successful this connection could be (Our Languages, 2012).

However, connections between the mainstream and complementary sectors are all too often seen as a one-way transmission of ideas. It is vital that learning takes place on both sides. Hall *et al* (2002) argue that complementary teachers should be recognised as 'transformative intellectuals' and recommend policymakers to engage in dialogue with complementary schools. Leena Robertson (2010) organised a groundbreaking project in which students in initial teacher education at a UK university visited complementary schools and reflected on the implications for their own teaching. This experience had a striking effect. The future teachers realised that community learning is significant, and that their pupils have important linguistic and cultural skills.

Our teacher partnership project took a step further by facilitating a two-way exchange of strategies between complementary and mainstream educators. For the first time, teachers from both sectors worked together in face-to-face partnership as equal colleagues. We describe the difference this made.

The teacher partnership project

The two-year project began with primary teachers visiting complementary schools in their neighbourhood and hosting return visits by teacher partners from those settings. Each complementary-mainstream partnership then worked collaboratively to plan and teach topic-based lessons, using strategies that enabled the children to develop their language skills in each context. In complementary school, most teachers were already working bilingually – as described earlier – since English was many pupils' stronger language. In primary school, teachers aimed to draw on the languages of all the children in the class, alongside English.

The study built on our previous bilingual learning research in Tower Hamlets, East London. Once again we worked closely with the Languages Service of the local education authority. Unusually for the UK, the local council makes some funding available for complementary schools and the Languages Service runs a one-year part-time teacher training course for complementary teachers in collaboration with a further education college, as well as termly professional development sessions. Bengali complementary schools are well established, because the predominant population of Tower Hamlets is of Bangladeshi origin, mostly settled for at least two generations. The borough also has a significant Somali population, recently arrived due to war and economic hardship in Somalia, who have begun setting up language classes. Many smaller language groups in the borough also run complementary schools, including newer arrivals from Eastern Europe. Our project involved Bengali, Somali and Russian schools, as these were some of the communities represented in the primary schools concerned.

Two primary schools participated; School A and School C. School A had been involved in our bilingual learning research (together with School B as discussed in Chapter 2), whilst School C had worked with our team in an earlier study of learning with grandparents. Four complementary schools were involved (two Bengali, one Somali and one Russian) plus on-site after-school Bengali and Somali classes at School A. Table 1 gives key details of each school.

Table 1: Participating schools

Primary School A	Pupils mainly Bangladeshi British. Class size 20-25.
After-school Bengali class at School A	Two days a week, 3.30-5 pm. 15 pupils aged 5-15.
After-school Somali class at School A	Two days a week, 3.30-5 pm. Started in response to parents' request when project began. 12 pupils aged 3-11, accompanied by parents.
Bengali Community School	Two blocks from School A, some pupils in common. Based in community centre, modern pre-fabricated building. 60 pupils aged 5-15 in 3 classes. Classes every weekday, 5-7 pm, in Bengali and Qur'anic Arabic.
Somali Community School	Two sites: old community hall (2 days a week, 5-7pm) and cramped community flat (Saturday and Sunday mornings). Each class 20 pupils aged 5-15.
Primary School C	Around half of pupils Bangladeshi British, others from a considerable mix of origins. Class size 20-25.
Bengali Mosque School	Some pupils in common with School C. On premises of Islamic secondary school. 160 pupils aged 6-13 in 8 classes. Classes every weekday, 5-7 pm, in Bengali and Qur'anic Arabic.
Russian Community School	Some pupils in common with School C. In rooms at a church with a Sunday service in Russian. 25 students aged 5-15 in 3 classes. Classes Sunday 12.30-1.30.

Eight teacher partnerships were set up, as shown in Table 2. Six involved School A, the larger primary school with greater staff capacity, and two involved School C.

Table 2: Teacher partnerships

Mainstream partner	Complementary partner
Annika (School A)	Sulaman (Bengali Community School)
Alison (School A)	Shah Ali (Bengali Community School)
James (School A)	Zainab (Somali Community School)
Siobhan (School A)	Muna (Somali Community School)
Shaheen (School A)	Rakib (School A Bengali class)
Jane (School A)	Osman (School A Somali class)
Hamida (School C)	Redwan (Bengali Mosque School)
Jo (School C)	Natasha and Tanya (Russian Community School)

Sulaman, headteacher of Bengali Community School, had founded the school ten years ago and developed the syllabus. His colleague Shah had several years experience and was attending the local authority's teacher training course, which Sulaman had completed some years before. Zainab and Muna had begun teaching at Somali Community School in the last couple of years, and were attending the local authority course. Rakib, a primary teacher at School A, taught Bengali both at the after-school class and as part of the mainstream curriculum. School A had instituted Bengali language lessons for all students because our previous research had revealed its importance for their intellectual and social development. Osman, who taught the after-school Somali class, had been a secondary school teacher of history and geography in Somalia. Redwan from Bengali Mosque School had attended training sessions at a local Muslim Centre. Natasha at Russian Community School had been a secondary school ICT teacher in Russia, whilst her colleague Tanya did not have previous teaching experience.

The mainstream teachers all had a number of years experience apart from James, the music and drama teacher in School A, who was planning to take a teacher training course to become a class teacher in the future. Some had knowledge of languages other than English. Annika spoke Swedish because her mother was from Sweden, whilst Shaheen and Hamida were from Bangladeshi families and spoke Bengali (Shaheen grew up in Bangladesh and

Hamida in London), and Jane had learnt some Arabic whilst working in Egypt.

Our research question was:

■ How can complementary-mainstream teacher partnerships develop pedagogies to enhance children's learning in both settings?

To launch the project, each primary school held an event to which they invited complementary school staff. Before teachers made individual visits to their partner's school, we interviewed everyone to find out whether they had ever visited the other setting prior to the project, and what they thought they might learn from each other. After the first visit, each partnership met to choose a topic and plan around it.

Planning sessions were held at the primary school to take advantage of resources there. Funding provided supply cover for the primary teachers and replacement salary for the complementary teachers, most of whom had weekday jobs. Partners then taught their first lesson, visiting each other to observe. A second planning session was held before teaching further lessons on the same theme or a new one, taking advantage of what had been learnt in the first action research cycle. During or after the partnership work, we interviewed the teachers to explore their responses.

Critical action research

We adopted a critical action research approach to challenge existing power structures and create a more equal relationship between teachers from the dominant mainstream system and the marginalised complementary sector. We wanted to help participants view the other setting in a new and different way. Complementary teachers needed to be aware of their strengths, otherwise they could be daunted by the knowledge that mainstream teachers had training and resources unavailable to them. We arranged for the mainstream teachers to visit complementary schools first, so that the complementary teachers were on their own ground where they would feel more confident. We devised the same initial interview questions and the same observation sheet for teachers from both sectors, rather than reinforcing the assumption that mainstream teachers had greater experience and their complementary partners more to learn.

In the interview we asked participants to tell us:

■ what they thought might differ between settings
■ what they would like to learn from their visit

■ what skills they would like to add to their teaching

■ how their partner teacher might be able to assist them

■ how they would like to help children use their mother tongue – or in the case of complementary teachers, were already doing so.

In the observation sheets we declared that 'children learn in many different ways' and suggested focusing on children's learning instead of the teaching methods used. We encouraged teachers to look for the strengths and interests the pupils showed, beginning with how children used community languages and English within the lesson – an inevitable advantage for complementary classes since other languages were rarely used in mainstream school. We asked them to observe how children helped each other or studied independently, how cultural knowledge was used, and the teacher/child and teacher/parent relationship. In these ways we highlighted the importance of social and cultural aspects of learning, changing the emphasis from the dominant view that good practice must necessarily include methods such as games, roleplay and investigative tasks. We took a similar approach to that of Leena Robertson, who set observation tasks focusing on the child as learner when her student teachers visited complementary schools, in order to 'shift teacher training students' longheld assumptions and perspectives' (Robertson, 2010: 124).

We present our findings here. First we discuss the teachers' views before the partnership work began. Then we explain how teaching approaches from the complementary sector provided new ideas for mainstream teachers, and vice versa. Finally, we offer one example: Somali teacher Zainab and mainstream teacher James are shown co-constructing a lesson that combined strategies from both settings.

The teachers' starting points

None of the mainstream teachers had visited a complementary school during their teacher training or teaching career. However, some made links with their childhood experiences of community learning. Annika and Hamida had attended complementary school, in Swedish and Bengali respectively. Both understood the importance of learning mother tongue and the challenges facing complementary teachers. Annika's class had included children with different levels of Swedish, whilst Hamida remembered traditional teaching methods but thought these might have changed by now. Jo referred to the benefits of Sunday school or drama classes, which had given her skills and confidence.

Several of the mainstream teachers imagined complementary school methods might be more formal and disciplined, particularly if there were large classes and few resources. Yet all had demonstrated their interest in complementary schools through volunteering to participate in the project, and some thought groupwork or experiential learning might be taking place there. Shaheen had taught a Bengali complementary class many years ago, and used methods picked up from her mother, who was a primary school teacher in the UK. She could see the value of linking mainstream and complementary schools.

Mainstream teachers were open to learning from their complementary school partners. Jo thought that sharing classroom strategies could refresh your ideas so you didn't get 'set in a bubble'. Others wondered if complementary teachers could draw on cultural knowledge to engage children in learning, particularly those whose behaviour was challenging. Annika had recently met complementary teachers when conducting a training session for the local authority, and found some to be 'incredibly intuitive' and 'aware how children will learn best'. She felt 'we shared a common understanding', and their awareness of children's bilingual resources was a special strength.

Complementary teachers' language knowledge was recognised as an advantage for the partnership work to come. Annika understood that mother tongue classes supported learning: 'I'm fully behind it, anything we can gather about how they're learning in language one should help inform their learning in language two'. Siobhan expected to see 'skills developing in mother tongue that you wouldn't see in school'.

Teachers wanted to bring these bilingual skills into the mainstream. Jane was concerned that the only Somali child in her class had no mother tongue support for her learning and hoped Osman, the Somali after-school teacher, could help her. Jo was keen to try bilingual strategies, such as a child reading in mother tongue and classmates trying to guess the meaning. Together with an Arabic-speaking parent, she had read a dual language storybook to a class in a previous teaching post. She thought her partnership with the Russian complementary school could help Sasha, the Russian-speaking child in her class, to lead a group task.

Alison looked forward to seeing new techniques for language and literacy teaching at complementary school, and wanted to find out about the grammatical structure of Bengali so she could understand how it affected children's learning of English. She had seen Rakib, who taught Bengali in the primary school, putting up keywords in Bengali to support children's learning, and wondered if she could do the same.

Hamida was well aware of the potential advantages of bilingual learning, thanks to her own experience of growing up in a Bangladeshi family and adding English at school. She explained that children 'grow their language [ie English] on their mother tongue language ... so in their head they are translating and they are using what they already know'. Thus by doing topic work in more than one language, children could build academic vocabulary in mother tongue. She herself had lost this opportunity because she only used Bengali in family contexts and English became her dominant language: 'you're forever speaking English'. However, despite her awareness, she was not currently teaching bilingually. She felt her partner teacher could help her with methods for learning and teaching Bengali.

Shaheen also understood how bilingual learning worked, from research findings and her own experience. She observed that if children compare words in different languages 'that helps them to memorise more, it's exercise for the brain'. She had used dual language teaching in primary school in the past, but 'it got lost somewhere' because she saw no other languages being used in school 'so I just thought, well nobody cares'. She did not think bilingual topic work would be time-consuming; 'it naturally can fit in, if you want it to'.

Meanwhile, none of the complementary teachers had visited a primary or secondary school as part of their work as a teacher, so they were just as unfamiliar with the mainstream setting. Some had been inside a primary school as parents, and remarked on the abundant resources and visual aids they saw there. Several noted other advantages such as having your own premises, training, and spending more time with pupils. They realised mainstream teaching approaches could be different. Redwan had heard about 'learning through play', whereas he taught in 'Bangladeshi style', and was keen to learn mainstream strategies. Osman was investigating UK teaching methods through BBC online materials. Tanya, who taught the youngest children in Russian school, was interested in approaches for early learning. She and Natasha, as new complementary teachers, saw mainstream schools as having more knowledge about children and their learning, whereas their school specialised in Russian language and culture. Natasha even referred to the mainstream as children's 'natural environment'.

The two most experienced complementary teachers had greater confidence in their own methodologies. Sulaman had been teaching for ten years and spoke eloquently about the approaches he had developed. He explained how he gave each child a task slightly above their level, to challenge them and stimulate their learning. This chimes perfectly with Vygotsky's concept of the zone of proximal development (Vygotsky, 1978), though Sulaman had figured out his approach on his own. He wrote songs and poems for children to study, encouraging them to express their ideas. He also emphasised children's need to move around during the class – 'when they're moving, their mind is moving' – which fits with the kinaesthetic learning approach. Sulaman considered there could be a two-way exchange of learning between himself and his mainstream partner. Sulaman's colleague Shah Ali thought the project would introduce an element of healthy competition: 'I will try and do my best to show my best and they will try their best and through this it will be very good for the students, they will learn lots of things.'

Only one teacher taught in both sectors. Rakib, an experienced class teacher at School A, now taught Bengali in the curriculum as well as after school. Rakib found some methods appropriate for both settings, such as using stories and rhymes. However, he pointed out that his after school class had a much wider range of ages and levels, 'so we have to concentrate on one-to-one teaching, we teach them according to their need'. He already used a topic work approach for his in-school Bengali teaching, linking it to curriculum themes. His vision was to further develop children's academic repertoire in Bengali: 'the second and third generation need to know the language [ie Bengali], so that's why they can use their mother tongue alongside English to study'.

Shah and Sulaman explained why they taught bilingually, using English as a bridge to mother tongue. Shah said 'here the first language for the children is English. ... I help them to understand through English, if I use only Bangla they don't always understand. I let them speak a little English and encourage them to speak Bangla'. Natasha recognised that 'I cannot teach Russian as I was taught at school ... I need to teach Russian as a second language'.

All the teachers were eager to begin the project, to find out about each other's classrooms and methods and share ideas. The partnership work was a venture into new territory. Below we consider what they found there, starting with teaching approaches in complementary school.

A strong teacher-student relationship

All the complementary teachers created a relationship with their students that was friendly yet firm. They negotiated discipline through warmth as well as strictness. Children hugged Zainab as they arrived in class, and this close relationship did not seem to be affected by her direct approach to instructions or reprimands. When her students misbehaved they had to stand facing the wall but they accepted this with good humour and continued to contribute to class discussion.

Redwan's chair and table were on a raised platform with a red carpet, showing the significance of his role as a teacher. He stressed, however, that it was important to have a friendly relationship with children, especially as they were tired after a day at mainstream school. He greeted the children respectfully with *asalaam aleikum*, and they responded in kind. In Sulaman and Shah's classes, the *salaam* greeting generated a similar atmosphere of mutual respect. Natasha's class was much smaller and she treated the children as part of a family. As she helped Sasha with his work, she put her arm round him and called him Sashka, the Russian diminutive for his name.

Mainstream teachers were impressed by the way the teachers and students in the complementary classes related to each other. Jo noted that children received more individual attention in the small classes at Russian school and that this helped them be relaxed and confident. Alison noted that children in Shah's class showed discipline, respect for learning and respect for the teacher. James said of the Somali teachers he observed that: 'their children have a lot of respect for them'.

Several teachers were struck by the way complementary teachers managed children with difficult behaviour, some of whom behaved similarly in mainstream school. For example, when Sulaman taught a mainstream class as part of the research, he quickly responded to children who might have become disruptive. He took them under his wing, inviting them to stand next to him and help him teach. This approach increased the children's self-esteem and they began to play a positive role in the class.

Teacher partners on the project found classroom management to be a shared concern. When discussing different behaviour strategies James, Zainab and Muna agreed it was a hard job being a teacher. Some strategies were common to both settings, as James realised when he saw children's hands go up to answer a question and guessed Zainab must have said in Somali: 'don't shout out'. The complementary teachers were able to base their approaches on a shared sense of community and cultural understanding, adapted to children growing up in the UK.

High expectations
The complementary teachers were determined all their students should succeed. Sulaman had developed a detailed curriculum for each level in his school and planned to make this even more challenging. He constantly en-

couraged his colleagues to explore new strategies and expect even more of students.

Zainab set demanding tasks, such as translating several sentences from English into Somali, and encouraged her students with cries of 'Come on!' in English until the task was completed. She and Muna made sure they heard each child demonstrate their learning, asking them to take turns to read out their own sentences in Somali or perform a song. Shah was concerned to see that when groupwork took place in a mainstream classroom, not all groups had to report back. In his view, this meant some could not consolidate their learning.

Sulaman, Shah and Muna set up friendly competitions between groups to motivate their students. Shah offered step by step support to a group who found a task particularly difficult, building their confidence by saying 'you are my stronger group' and 'you think you can't but you can', and offering to reward them if they did well.

High standards were expected at complementary school events where students performed for families and the community, and teachers and students spent much time and energy preparing. In Bengali Mosque School, every single one of the 160 students performed at the whole school assembly. Students from Bengali Community School rehearsed over and over again for the Tower Hamlets Languages Celebration, making their own costumes and props with materials brought from home. In comparison, their companion group from School A had to fit practice into fragmented moments in the school day. Annika was impressed by the efforts made at complementary school and noted ruefully that the mainstream curriculum left little space for children to develop their work in this way.

Complementary schools could devise their own marking systems, which gave some flexibility in assessment. Sulaman used this freedom to motivate students, offering them the chance to get a higher mark by attempting a more difficult task. He sometimes gave a better mark than a student strictly deserved, just a few points away from the top, so as to encourage them to strive even harder next time. Flexibility did not mean achievement was taken lightly, however. Natasha discussed with Sasha why he had not got the top mark of five for that day's work, explaining exactly what he needed to do to obtain it.

Rapid feedback to pupils was considered important. Zainab marked each child's spelling test on the spot while her pupils did another task. James commented on the children's eagerness as they waited for their results, and how they appreciated instant evaluation. Jo was surprised when a parent at Russian school complained to her that his children put effort into homework at primary school but it was marked late or not at all, whereas they were given immediate feedback from their complementary teachers. Every community's dedication to their children's success was evident through the teaching, assessment and performance taking place in complementary school.

Teachers and students exchanging knowledge

Complementary teachers needed to work together with their students to facilitate learning, because the teachers were expert in mother tongue and the students in English. To negotiate understanding in class, both languages were used. When Zainab taught new vocabulary in Somali, she always asked for the English translation, and discussed different possible meanings with her students. When she wrote the English word on the board, children would prompt her, for example by sounding out the individual letters that spelt 'tea', or explaining that 'pizza' began with 'p' not 'b' (sounds that were difficult for Zainab to distinguish). Similarly, children in Redwan's class corrected his spelling of 'shef' to 'chef'.

Yet students maintained respect for the teacher, as James had noted. Having seen Zainab cheerfully admit she did not know everything and needed support, he realised he could ask his students for help when his dyslexia gave him difficulties with spelling. Jo too thought a more equal teacher-student relationship could be beneficial. After Sasha had explained to her how to write letters of the alphabet at Russian school, she said to him: 'it makes a change, doesn't it Sasha, when you know more than me!'

Children's responsibility for learning and teaching

Because many complementary classes included students of different ages and levels, teachers often organised children to work on tasks independently or lead a small group. In Redwan's class, each child practised the Bengali alphabet letters they were currently learning. Some rehearsed by themselves, reciting silently or aloud, whilst others worked in twos or threes, taking it in turns to test their peers by listening. When ready, they put their hands up and Redwan came to check their learning.

Muna arranged her multi-age class into groups for some activities, with the more advanced students as leaders. Rakib's class had a wide range of learners, from a nine-year-old reading stories in Bengali to a 14-year-old who was a complete beginner. Having assigned appropriate tasks, Rakib circulated responding to requests for help.

After observing Sulaman's pupils working in pairs and groups, Annika commented that children were not asked to be such independent learners in primary school. The challenging conditions in complementary school required children to develop their concentration and self-motivation.

A child might also teach the whole class. Sulaman asked ten-year-old Rafia to take over whilst he dealt with some administrative tasks, and she set up her own list of points on the whiteboard which she then proceeded to explain. Zainab and Muna began their lessons by writing ten Somali words on the board and children learnt through recitation, led firstly by the teacher and then each student. The children waited eagerly for their opportunity, knowing that everyone would have a turn. They led their peers with confidence, using a dramatic voice and varying intonation. Each child focused on a particular aspect that interested them, such as the exact pronunciation of a long vowel sound.

James found the 'child as teacher' strategy very effective:

> It's a more rounded use of resources, it develops the children in different ways – self-learning, self-monitoring ... the understanding you get from having to teach something, to try to explain it, focusing in your head on what it should be.

His description echoes Eve Gregory's analysis of the synergy operating between siblings learning together (Gregory, 2001). In complementary school, children are similarly exchanging ideas through peer teaching. In addition, each child shares some responsibility for the learning of the whole group. Whenever children presented work in Zainab's class, others would join in with corrections and everyone would clap. As James put it, complementary classes operate as learning communities where 'everyone puts something in'.

Bilingual strategies

Most complementary teachers used English as a bridge to help children access the community language, and explored meanings through translation. Like Sulaman, Shah and Rakib, Redwan switched between Sylheti (the children's spoken variety), Standard Bengali and English to aid understanding. If a child made use of the English system – for example, suggesting 'Jamaica' when asked for a country name beginning with a Bengali letter sounding similar to the English 'J' – he would acknowledge the idea and explain the difference.

In Arabic classes another language was added for meaning-making. Pupils in Sulaman's class recited a story from the Qur'an which featured the Arabic word for elephant, *fil*. Sulaman asked what it meant and children made suggestions based on English: 'feeling your hand' or 'filling the gap'. Laughing, Sulaman said: 'three languages we are learning'. He explained *fil* in Arabic meant elephant and asked them for the Bengali word too, which a child supplied: *hati*.

Zainab's class discussed different meanings when they were translating words which had a cultural basis. One Somali word meant something like a 'hot water bottle', but was this the same as the English item or was it a jug used for hot water? Was a 'sleeping mat' similar to a 'sleeping bag'? Teacher and children went to and fro between the two languages as they negotiated the meaning, and made a final decision on what to write on the board in English.

Zainab likewise encouraged children to build ideas in English to understand a Somali song. This led to complex thinking; a phrase involving the Somali words *aqoon* (knowledge) and *iftiin* (light or brightness) produced suggestions such as 'your knowledge is bright' and 'your brain shines a light on the darkness'.

Developing bilingual work in partnership

Teacher partners planned together to explore how bilingual strategies could be used in primary school as well as complementary class. In mainstream classrooms, children could draw on their own languages and learn about each other's. Shah and Alison used stories in more than one language. One was The Buri and the Marrow in Bengali and English, with a parallel story The Old Woman and the Red Pumpkin in English. Another was the Pied Piper dual language storybook in Bengali and English, and Somali and English. In Alison's class, children wrote playscripts including words and phrases in different languages which they chose for effect. Shah asked his students to write the story in English as a basis for further study in Bengali.

Natasha, Tanya and Jo also worked with parallel stories: *Kolobok* in Russian was a little ball of dough whose sad ending was very similar to that of the Gingerbread Man in English. The children listened to the stories in both versions and worked out what was happening. Then they role-played particular scenes in each language and in English, building their vocabulary bilingually.

Redwan and Hamida chose the Noah's Ark story, which children also encountered in their Qur'anic studies, to focus on animal vocabulary. Pupils from Hamida's multilingual class took a worksheet of animal pictures home to ask parents for words in other languages. Redwan's students used the same sheet to generate Bengali and English words.

These teacher partners also worked on 'Jobs in different countries', using photos from Bangladesh as a stimulus for ideas. Both the older children in Redwan's class and the young pupils in Hamida's nursery class drew on experiences in Bangladesh to suggest words they knew, and learned new ones in English as well as Bengali. Hamida and Redwan used the vocabulary to compare initial phonemes in Bengali and English.

Osman and Jane took the theme of food. A Somali parent helped children in Jane's nursery class make *laxoox* bread, and Jane and Osman used shared writing in English and Somali to scribe children's memories of the experience, recalled by photos. Osman's class enjoyed *laxoox* bread with accompanying meat and vegetables, then brainstormed words for the ingredients in Somali. A successful gardening session was held with children and parents at School A, for Osman's Somali class, Rakib's after-school Bengali class, and Shaheen's Year 1 class. The children learned parallel vocabulary in three languages as they planted vegetables.

Somali has the same script as English, but Bengali and Russian each have different orthography. Transliteration into Roman script was a key strategy for enabling teachers and children who knew no Bengali or Russian to work with texts in these languages. Sulaman and Annika compared a Bengali poem to an English one on a similar theme. To fully understand the poem, Sulaman's pupils as well as Annika's needed a transliteration of the complex literary language in Bengali, and a translation into English. By working with the three versions alongside each other, the children in both classes could build meanings. Sulaman encouraged his students to attempt tasks in Bengali script, transliterated Bengali or Sylheti, or English – or all of them. He characterised this approach as learning 'in between', saying that 'once they do all those, it will stay in their mind'. Children's thinking was given maximum support because they could generate ideas by translating between languages, and doing this reinforced concepts and made for a rich learning experience.

Annika's pupils of Bangladeshi origin wrote questions in transliterated Sylheti or Bengali so they could talk at home with parents about the poem. Students who did not speak Bengali showed the English version to parents and asked if they knew similar poems in other languages. They brought songs in Arabic and transliterated Urdu to class, and one child, helped by his father, translated the original poem into Spanish. Annika was at first disconcerted when she was planning for children to use Bengali, telling us: 'I feel de-skilled!'. But she quickly realised her role was to act as facilitator, to allow the children to take their multilingual learning forward.

The partnership work added to the complementary teachers' bilingual strategies as well. Sulaman and Shah had always used transliteration, but now it became a stronger element in their work. They used it judiciously, giving students differentiated tasks to ensure they progressed to developing Bengali script. The new complementary teachers, Osman, Natasha and Tanya, began to use English as well as Somali or Russian in their teaching. Having observed children learning bilingually in project activities in mainstream class, they realised how English could act as a resource for their pupils together with mother tongue.

The mainstream teachers began to use or develop their own language expertise by taking part in the project. Shaheen rapidly created ideas in Bengali with her project partner, Rakib. They had been colleagues teaching in the same primary school for years but this was their first chance to devise bilingual lessons together. Rakib introduced Shaheen to the Bengali font on the school computer system, and she began to make bilingual worksheets.

Annika taught her class a song in Swedish, to their mutual delight. Jane drew on her knowledge of Arabic when working with Osman, since Arabic is also spoken in Somalia and was part of his lessons. Alison revealed she was half Italian and wished she had learnt the language as a child. However, through taking part in project activities with her class, she began to learn some Bengali for the first time in her teaching career, and noted that 'I was thinking in English and Bangla for some of the words'.

Groupwork, games and role-play

These approaches are common in mainstream schools and complementary teachers also found them helpful. Some were already employing such strategies. Groupwork was often used in complementary school to deal with mixed level classes, as described earlier. Rakib brought his mainstream experience into his Bengali classes, and several complementary teachers had acquired ideas from local authority training or devised their own strategies. For others, these techniques were new and offered additional possibilities. All the complementary teachers developed their approaches further through interacting with mainstream partners as they planned topic-based work together.

When Zainab organised her class into groups to investigate the meaning of a Somali song, she was pleased at the good results of telling children to 'ask your friends'. Redwan devised a discussion task around photos of Bangladesh, with one child as scribe for each group, and the children worked conscientiously to produce Bengali words describing the pictures.

Osman observed learning through play in Jane's nursery class, and on her advice he divided his Somali class into an older and a younger group and gave them differentiated activities. The younger group sorted plastic models of fruit and vegetables into those grown in England or those grown in Somalia, while older children produced a Venn diagram in which they wrote vocabulary for each category and identified items grown in both countries. The two groups then came together and played a memory game to revise the new words they had learned.

Natasha and Tanya benefited from using a hands-on approach with their partner teacher Jo, in which the children developed vocabulary and narrative skills through roleplays based on the Kolobok story. Natasha noted that 'if they're active, they learn better', while Tanya talked of learning 'the creative way'. Both teachers incorporated these strategies into their lessons, encouraging children to imagine the Kolobok character meeting a new set of animals in Africa, or having to dress up in different clothes to protect himself from rain. They used the topic to develop Russian literacy, by labelling animal pictures from the story (see Figure 9) or practising initial letters in words for clothes. Natasha reported that: 'I learned lots of methods and techniques from primary school teachers which I adopted and now use in my work'.

Sulaman and Shah already used differentiated groupwork and games in their classes. They gained the additional dimension of exploring a topic through a range of activities to develop different skills. As Shah pointed out, 'it's what they can do with one story, how they learn the words, to do role plays, how to answer questions, how to make speeches.' He was accustomed to using games such as wordsearches or Word Bingo for Bengali literacy, and the children responded with even greater enthusiasm when he adapted these to the topic.

Complementary teachers who encountered mainstream lesson planning for the first time understood the principles and rapidly learnt how to apply them. Osman wrote lesson plans in Somali, setting out the learning intention, success criteria, resources, key vocabulary, key skills, introductory activity, main activity differentiated for different groups, and plenary to revise learning. He used the section on 'role of support staff' – the teaching assistants in mainstream school – to plan ways of involving the parents, as they were with their children at his class.

Tanya began her lesson plan on 'Dressing up Kolobok' with the children learning the Russian words for clothes they were wearing. She used vocabulary flashcards for further practice, and the children then reinforced their

Figure 9: Writing animal names in Russian

learning by composing sentences with the new words and drawing clothes for characters in the story.

Interweaving strategies

The equal exchange of strategies between complementary and mainstream teachers was summed up by Shah:

> I liked lots of things and understood a lot of what they do. ... I can work comparatively with them, that is what I liked, that I could show very well my work and they were happy too, they also said they learnt from us, that was my wish.

Here we show an example of teachers combining strategies from both the settings. James co-taught a Year 6 class in primary school with Somali teachers Zainab and Muna. Their topic was a song well known in Somalia, *Arday baan ahay* (I am a student), about a child running eagerly to school to learn so they can contribute to their country (Figure 10). Table 3 shows how the teachers switched between strategies during the lesson. The complementary strategies were typical of Zainab's and Muna's Somali classes described earlier, whilst James used the mainstream strategies in his role as music and drama teacher.

When he presented his Somali colleagues to the class, James introduced them as equals by saying 'we're teaching buddies.' With Zainab and Muna's help, James had identified a list of Somali keywords from the song and had written them on a poster on the wall. Zainab led the first class recitation, emphasising

I am a student

I am a student, I am a student
I am the flower of this country!
I am running, running to
Attend my school
So I can establish who I am
And benefit my country
I have come to work hard
My God guide me through
My God guide me through
Amen, Amen.

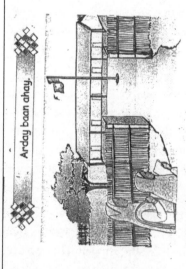

Arday baan ahay.

Arday baan ahayoo, arday baan ahayoo
Ubaxii waddankaan ahayoo!
Waxa aan u ordayaa, ordayaa
Dugsida la aadaa
Inaan aqoon kororsadoo
Dhulkayga anfacoo
Dadaalkii la imiyee
Allahayoow igu gargaar
Igu gargaar, allahayoow igu gargaar
Aamiin, Aamiin.

Arday baan ahayoo, arday baan ahayoo
Iftiinkii waddankaan ahayoo
Waxa aan u ordayaa, ordayaa
Imtixaanka u galaa
Inaan adduunka oo idil
Wixii jira ogaadoo
Dadaalkii la imiyee
Allahayoow igu gargaar
Aamiin, Aamiin.

Figure 10: Somali song 'I am a student'

86

Table 3: Strategies used for co-teaching

Complementary strategy	Mainstream strategy
reciting keywords	
correcting pronunciation	
child as teacher	
negotiating translation	
children help with spelling	
	drama to practise meaning
high expectations for behaviour	
	split into 2 groups, each learn half of song
	fine-tune performance
child as leader with support	

the correct pronunciation, and James led the second one. Then several children, including Abdilahi, one of the two Somali children in the class, enthusiastically took turns as teacher. Abdilahi helped again with discussing the meanings of the words. James wrote the English translations on the poster, and the children corrected him when he mis-spelled a word, just as children in Zainab's class would help her with English spelling. He accepted their help, reminding them he was dyslexic and saying that nobody is perfect.

James then used drama to help children understand and remember the keywords. Small groups chose Somali words to include in English sentences and act out: for example 'the *arday* went to the *dugsida*' (the student went to school). The children demonstrated their creative bilingual phrases to the whole class.

Before he handed over to Zainab and Muna to teach the song, James reminded the children about the expectations for behaviour in complementary school: 'Their students have a lot of respect for them ... so I don't want to have to tell you to stop talking when they're talking'. As Zainab and Muna began, James realised the song needed to be broken down into smaller chunks of language because the children were unfamiliar with Somali, so he modelled this approach. He made the task even more manageable by splitting the class into two groups, each to learn half of the song. As a music teacher, James emphasised the quality of singing. High standards for performance are, as we have seen, also typical of complementary school. When the two groups combined to sing the whole song, Zainab asked for a leader from each group, prompting them and supporting their singing when needed.

The children remembered the keywords at the end of the lesson, and offered appropriate ideas about the possible meanings of each line in the song. With help from the children and adults who spoke Somali, the class managed to understand the whole text. The combined strategies led to an extremely effective lesson in which the children actively participated to negotiate meaning and learn new language. The group maximised their resources by working bilingually and switching roles between teachers and students so that the class became a learning community to which everyone could contribute. Co-teaching was conducted seamlessly and with mutual understanding. James recognised the value of complementary teachers having different strategies that could add to mainstream teaching, saying: 'it isn't what you do, and that's why it's good for you to see it.'

Our findings show that teacher partners collaborated productively to exchange strategies. Complementary teachers demonstrated particular expertise through informal yet respectful relationships with pupils, encouraging children to take responsibility for their own learning and that of others in the class, and employing a range of bilingual strategies adapted to the students' needs. Complementary classes operated as learning communities in which teachers and students worked together to help everyone succeed. Through observation and discussion, the primary teachers gained understanding of children's potential as learners and began to develop multilingual pedagogies adapted to their own classes. Meanwhile, some complementary teachers were already using approaches often found in the mainstream, such as group-work, games and drama, and others quickly incorporated them into their repertoire. The teachers planned jointly to co-construct lessons that fruitfully combined strategies from both settings. In the next chapter, we focus on the curriculum content the teacher partners produced, which enabled children to draw on the full range of their multilingual resources for learning.

Ideas for developing learning strategies

■ Can you arrange to visit a local complementary school and invite the teachers there to visit you too? Parents will be able to put you in touch with complementary schools their children attend. Local authorities may also know about classes in your area and there is a directory of complementary schools on the website of the National Resource Centre for Supplementary Education at: http://www.continyou.org.uk/what_we_do/supplementary_education/

When visiting each other, what different strategies can mainstream and complementary partners observe that support children's learning? If mainstream schools invite complementary teachers to join professional development sessions, further sharing of ideas can take place.

■ Consider how your class can be strengthened as a learning community in which children are responsible for their own learning and that of others:

The child as teacher

Can children take it in turns to act as the teacher for the whole class? Children can also lead a small group in an activity on which they are more expert, or rotate leadership on different occasions. Being the leader helps children develop their thinking about the point they are teaching, as well as enhancing their self-confidence.

The child as independent learner

Are children given ownership of tasks to undertake individually, and do they have sufficient time to complete them? Are the goals challenging enough and do all children know they are expected to perform to a high level? Can children set their own targets for what they want to achieve? Does each child have the opportunity to demonstrate their learning to the teacher or the class?

The learning community

When children are preparing a task independently, can peers help by checking each other's learning and giving advice? When the class is working together as a whole group, are children encouraged to collaborate to correct each other and clarify understanding? Are children's families part of the learning community so they can build a meaningful connection to the task?

Teachers and students exchanging knowledge

Inviting children to share their linguistic and cultural resources in class leads to a more equal teacher-student relationship. Children will be the experts and enjoy helping you learn, whilst also developing their own capabilities as they translate and explain.

■ Examples of partnership work from the research project show how complementary and mainstream teachers developed strategies to enhance children's learning. These are available on the Goldsmiths Multilingual Learning webpages at: http://www.gold.ac.uk/clcl/multilingual-learning/cmp/

4

Connecting the Curriculum

It's about the whole child really ... just by having contact with their community schools I feel I can understand a bit more about their learning in a broader context – they've got skills we don't always use in class and doing the poetry work has given us the chance to use some of those skills ... it was lovely to see the confidence of the children who were able to take on the task and engage with it, using their mother tongue.

This is how Annika summed up the benefits of a week of successful literacy lessons for her primary school class on Bengali and English poetry. She had planned it together with Sulaman, her teacher partner from Bengali complementary school, and both found that the partnership enriched their teaching. The traditional Bengali poem *Kajla Didi* conjured up the beauty of the natural world in a village environment well known to parents and grandparents, and often visited by the children too. The theme of a beloved older sister gone missing evoked the universal experience of loss, paralleled in the English poem 'What Has Happened to Lulu'. The two poems were used together to inspire children's writing in Bengali and English.

Annika was struck by the children's enthusiastic response to the Bengali poem and how their families became involved in their learning. The poem was taken home overnight and almost every child in the class discussed it with their parents or grandparents, one even making a special visit to his grandmother on that cold December evening. All the adults recognised *Kajla Didi* and a family connection was forged through sharing it together. One child commented: 'My dad said this poem is really old and he read it when he was a little kid like us right now'.

Kajla Didi was available in three versions: Bengali script, Bengali transliterated into Roman letters, and English translation. This made the meaning accessible to everyone, including families who were not from Bangladeshi backgrounds. The children had studied the poem in class and composed questions for their parents in transliterated Bengali or English. Annika encouraged them to bring back other poems from home, so the children recited Arabic and Urdu poetry and acted a short Bengali play. One boy had translated *Kajla Didi* into Spanish with his father's help. The bilingual poetry work revealed knowledge and capacities that were formerly hidden. Annika complimented her class, saying 'You're all very talented children' and they responded in the words of a popular TV show 'We've got talent!'

The range of topics generated by the poem led children into a wider world of learning that spanned literary heritage, natural history, social practices in different cultures, and linguistic knowledge. Sulaman's class worked in groups to devise questions about *Kajla Didi* and, like Annika's students, they investigated the flora and fauna of Bangladesh mentioned in the poem. What exactly was the 'bamboo garden' bathed in moonlight, why did the flowers of the lemon tree smell so strong that they kept the little girl awake, and how do fireflies shine? They explored cultural practices such as the 'dolls' wedding' game that the girl remembered playing with her sister, and wanted to know if boys played it too? They learned by sharing the ideas they brought from home.

A child who was newly-arrived from Bangladesh became central in Annika's class, using his expertise in Bengali to help interpret the poem and co-write bilingually with his peers. Sulaman observed this when visiting the class, saying: 'in the writing, he expressed himself and he got confidence in the class ... he got something and he felt proud of it'.

Sulaman's presence supported other children to begin writing in Bengali script and other languages, demonstrating the knowledge they had gained from complementary school. Annika learnt more about children's language skills by watching the students in Sulaman's class switch between Sylheti, Bengali and English to make sense of the poetry work.

The theme of losing a member of your family spoke deeply to children and gained additional resonance when also expressed in the English poem 'What Has Happened to Lulu', by Charles Causley (1975:226). The children drew on both poems in their writing, responding to imagery such as Lulu's empty bed and the curtain flapping at her open window, and the mother who covered her head and turned away when asked about Kajla Didi. Their writing echoed phrases from English and Bengali, capturing the rhythm of the original poetry to develop ideas from their personal experience. One child imagined losing a younger sibling in a fairground, whilst another expressed grief about the death of a stillborn brother. Incorporating Arabic words in transliteration, as in one child's title '*Mahbub hua da'ir!*' (Mahbub he is lost!), showed how the children were making links with their home worlds.

Annika noted how this multilingual and multicultural curriculum tapped into fundamental aspects of children's lives so that they felt 'proud of who they are'. She saw this as 'a very important part of the work, their pride and self-esteem, it was about acknowledging who they are as individuals'. Sulaman gave his view on the importance of engaging families: 'sharing to learn better, it's a little guide from the home, I think it's wonderful'.

In complementary school, the bilingual poetry work further developed characteristic features such as strong home-school relationships and children using their wider linguistic and cultural skills. In the primary school, Annika discovered the complexity of her students' knowledge and asserted that school should be 'a place where we acknowledge the broad skills that children have'. She recognised the advantages of bringing bilingual learning into the mainstream, commenting that 'obviously English is what we're being asked to teach but what I think I learned from this is that children who are actually being very successful in English seem to also be children who are engaging with mother tongue classes as well'.

The work of Sulaman and Annika demonstrates how cultural knowledge from students' homes and communities can be a springboard for learning. This contrasts with the prevalent view that children from ethnic minority backgrounds gain knowledge of the wider world by coming to mainstream school. Many primary school teachers have told our research team that 'we need to provide a rich experience for children here, because they have so little at home'. By researching in homes we have shown the contrary to be true; for example, some young children's knowledge of plant growth from gardening with grandparents far exceeds the targets of the school science curriculum (Ruby *et al*, 2007).

Misunderstandings by mainstream teachers are partly based on their lack of experience of community learning. But such views also stem from placing a low value on knowledge from other cultures, in a viewpoint that is essentially colonialist. A secondary school teacher recently told one of our colleagues: 'these students' experience is quite restricted – they've never been further than Bangladesh'. It is unlikely he would have made the same remark if students had visited a European country or the United States. Bangladesh, it seems, does not count as a source of learning.

In this chapter we explain how researchers and educators have emphasised the benefits of a curriculum drawing on home and community knowledge. However, teachers often find this difficult to put into practice because minority languages and cultures are excluded from mainstream school at an institutional level. Meanwhile, complementary schools operate in marginalised spaces and have little official recognition, but their teachers have greater flexibility to devise a curriculum appropriate to their students' needs. We argue that although mainstream schools have institutional power, complementary schools are spaces where greater *learning power* can be developed.

We go on to give examples from our research showing what happened when complementary teachers took the lead in bringing the wider world into mainstream school. Their holistic perspective broadened and deepened learning, enabling children and their families to participate actively with teachers in shaping a multilingual and multicultural curriculum. As part of this process, mainstream teachers gained support to draw on their own linguistic and cultural resources. By working together on an equal basis, complementary and mainstream teachers disrupted institutional power structures, creating conditions under which they could maximise *learning power* instead.

Challenges for a multicultural curriculum

Families from linguistic minority backgrounds possess 'funds of knowledge' gained from everyday experience, according to Luis Moll and colleagues (1992). As teacher-researchers working with Mexican-American families in Arizona, these authors successfully devised a curriculum drawing on parental expertise. Researchers and educators around the world have built on home and community resources within mainstream school. They have, to name only a few examples: created a multilingual literacy environment in a nursery class in London (Kenner, 2000); brought the knowledge of Māori elders into a New Zealand school (Glynn and Berryman, 2003); set up a language awareness project led by minority families in France (Young and Hélot, 2008); and introduced a science curriculum drawing on indigenous knowledge systems in Alaska (Barnhardt and Kawagley, 2005).

But when educators try to introduce a multilingual and multicultural approach they often encounter significant setbacks. Student teachers in London who were hoping to put into practice their ideals of a curriculum addressing ethnic diversity, for example through including historical figures from ethnic minority backgrounds in the topic of Victorian Britain, discovered there was little interest from colleagues since knowledge from outside the dominant culture was considered unimportant (Pearce, forthcoming). Researchers on a language awareness project in an Irish primary school found teachers were constrained by a curriculum that prioritised English and made it difficult to devote time to other languages (O'Rourke, 2011). Bilingual assistants in English primary schools could have used their students' languages as part of the curriculum, but were 'silenced' because their experience was ignored in the classroom (Robertson *et al*, under review).

The mainstream school system has the power to devalue and exclude linguistic and cultural knowledge that does not fit the norm. Jim Cummins (2001) talks of 'coercive power relations' operating in school that marginalise multilingualism. The National Curriculum in England, planned by the Conservative government in the late 1980s, makes almost no reference to languages and cultures other than English. David Gillborn (2005) argues that part of its aim was to maintain the values of the white British elite. A recent curriculum review (Ajegbo, 2007) recommended broader topic-based learning that would integrate multicultural experience, and links between the mainstream and community-based education such as complementary schools, but these suggestions have not been implemented.

Researchers and educators who work from a critical multiculturalist standpoint (May, 1999) emphasise the need to explicitly challenge the status quo at an institutional level in order to make structural changes. Sonia Nieto and Patti Bode (2008:xx) describe a new multicultural curriculum as 'education that affirms diversity, encourages critical thinking, and leads to social justice and action'. But how can individual teachers negotiate their way through existing power relationships to promote this kind of curriculum in mainstream schools?

Power is not necessarily monolithic. According to philosopher Michel Foucault (1980), we are all implicated in exercising and resisting power. This suggests that teachers do have agency to create new ways of relating to students in their classrooms. Cummins (2001) explains how educators working in multilingual settings can use power positively instead of negatively. By interacting with their students, teachers construct an 'interpersonal space' where identities can be negotiated and knowledge can be generated. Often 'coercive power relations' operate in this space, but if teachers work together with students on a more equal basis, this will generate 'collaborative power relations' instead, leading to 'transformative pedagogy'. The multiliteracies approach developed by Cummins and colleagues in Canada and elsewhere shows how students can create 'identity texts' that relate curriculum content to their individual and collective experience (Cummins and Early, 2011). Jean Conteh and Avril Brock (2011) have also argued for the need to construct 'safe spaces' in which bilingual learning can be developed, where multiple aspects of cultural experience can co-exist and interact to make new meanings.

Because it is difficult to create a multicultural curriculum that differs from institutional demands, mainstream educators are likely to require support from beyond the school itself. Patisepa Tuafuti and John McCaffery (2005) demonstrate that a collaborative empowerment approach must involve families and communities, through their example of Samoan bilingual schooling in New Zealand which has proved successful. Links with community educators could also be key. The particular strengths of complementary schools as flexible spaces for developing children's learning are now explored.

Complementary schools as sites of *learning power*

Recent research shows that complementary teachers tend to understand their students' multiple linguistic and cultural lifeworlds, and often try to integrate these experiences into their pedagogy through a holistic approach. Uvanney Maylor and colleagues (2010) surveyed complementary education in the UK and found that teachers built strong relationships with children and parents, responded flexibly to students' needs and fostered positive learner identities. Jim Anderson (2008) describes how London complementary teachers took a humanistic perspective to learning, designing their own curricula including literature, music and historical issues. Primary school teachers in Bradford set up Saturday complementary classes as spaces where they could draw on the children's different languages to explore concepts and skills related to the mainstream curriculum (Conteh, 2010).

Studies on complementary schooling in other countries demonstrate that teachers adopt similar approaches, which are grounded in close connections with their communities. Kathy Hall and co-researchers (2002) discovered that complementary schools in Norway had strong parental and community involvement. Teachers made links to mainstream curriculum topics while helping pupils to develop their different understandings and values by tapping into their multicultural heritage, which was too often ignored at mainstream school. This approach made education 'emotional, spiritual and deeply meaningful' (*ibid*:409) for those students. Chinese teachers in the US were found by Wu *et al* (2011:53) to be providing 'reciprocal, supportive and culturally relevant instruction'.

Clearly, then, complementary teachers have relative freedom to construct their own curriculum, basing their ideas on their understandings of students' linguistic and cultural background. This is why we argue that complementary schools can generate what we have called *learning power* even though they do not possess the institutional power of the mainstream system. Teachers, students and parents demonstrate greater agency in complementary settings because they are all able to participate in the education taking place there. Our definition of *learning power* involves working together as a community, co-constructing knowledge that draws on multilingual and multicultural resources.

Currently, examples of *learning power* are still rare in mainstream schools. However, researchers have pointed out that complementary teachers could become partners with mainstream teachers to co-design curricula, since they bring a wealth of knowledge about the ways children's language, culture and identity can be used positively in learning, and have strong links with parents and communities (Issa and Williams, 2009; Robertson, 2010). It is instructive to look at how teacher partners collaborated in our research to explore the potential of community-led approaches to the curriculum.

Valuing community resources

An incident that happened at the very beginning of the research highlights how complementary teachers can undervalue their own resources compared to the apparent advantages of mainstream schools. When the headteacher of one of the complementary schools in our study visited the primary school for the first time, he felt overwhelmed by the rich resources there. Back at his own school, he gestured at his rundown premises with their basic materials and told the researchers 'here we have nothing'. We were worried that the visit might reinforce his sense of marginalisation, so the Bangladeshi British member of our team, drawing on her own experience and understanding, explained that 'the children are your resources'. The headteacher's self-confidence was restored as we discussed the cultural knowledge that enabled him and his staff to interact positively with children and parents and provide his students with significant learning experiences.

Our initial interviews showed primary teachers were aware that complementary schools could bring value to children's learning. They recognised the important links with the children's home background, which tended to be lacking in mainstream school. James thought complementary teachers would give children a sense of their family history and culture, 'someone who knows the bits of you and what you've done'. In this way they could bridge the gap between different parts of the children's lives, whereas primary school could often feel alien. Charlotte noted that when children were from a similar cultural background to the teacher, 'you kind of know a bit more about what that other part of the child is, but when it's such a different cultural background to your own ... you're quite in the dark about that really'. She was keen to visit the complementary school because 'it would be really nice for me to see some of our children in a different context ... whether they are the same children we know here or very different'.

The teachers realised that complementary schools could help children build more secure cultural identities. Jo felt it was very important for children to keep links with their home culture and be with peers from a similar background, whereas in mainstream school they might be the only child speaking that particular language in their class. Jane was concerned that a Somali child in her class felt isolated, and hoped that her partner teacher Osman, from the on-site Somali class, could mediate a closer relationship with parents. Some teachers referred to their own childhood experiences; Hamida valued the social skills she had developed with friends at Bengali class. Annika remembered how learning Swedish with her grandmother had helped her identify with that aspect of her cultural heritage. She often had conversations with parents about the significance of cultural and linguistic roots, and how children would want to take their own decisions about constructing their multiple identities.

Several teachers commented that the mainstream curriculum failed to take account of cultural and linguistic diversity. Annika pointed out 'they've changed our curriculum from language to literacy, and *English* literacy – there was a time when we were much broader'. She remembered asking parents how children used languages at home, whereas such information was no longer collected. She thought the current curriculum felt 'stressed', with little opportunity for creativity. Alison realised that the children were seldom asked to bring their home language and culture into learning, and 'it would be nice to think more like that'. Charlotte wanted to make her lessons inclusive for all, for example by relating geography topics to different countries, 'so we do try to reach out a little bit, but I can honestly say I don't really use their first language in my teaching currently'. She remarked that 'we do try really hard to involve the parents and involve the community', but wondered whether parents would be more involved at complementary school.

Though they identified the difficulties, the teachers also saw potential for change and hoped the project would help to effect this. James thought the curriculum could include different languages to link children's home and school lives and give them a greater sense of ownership. Annika had conducted a language survey in her own class and noticed how 'children's shoulders went back' because they were proud of their linguistic expertise. Jo saw languages as a 'different talent that children have', which could help develop skills in a completely different way. She thought it would be 'an awesome thing' for her only Russian-speaking pupil to bring his culture into the classroom. This would give her more understanding of his life so she could build a better relationship with him. She suggested some ways that cultural exchange could take place in her class, for example by inviting Russian-speaking and Bengali-speaking parents to tell versions of the same story.

The research project planned to use topic-based work to develop new approaches to the curriculum, and teachers saw this as a potential way forward. Hamida began to consider how the current topic for her nursery class, 'People who help us', could be broadened. Like many of her pupils, she spoke Bengali and reflected that children's language skills could be used to learn about the topic: 'Can we go and do something in Bengali with that?' She thought bilingual learning would support the children's development of Bengali alongside English, since they would not necessarily encounter academic language in Bengali at home.

Charlotte realised multilingual work could be built into the curriculum, for example by focusing on key vocabulary in different languages. She had experienced this when working with Rakib, her primary teacher colleague at School A, who taught Bengali language lessons in mainstream school as well as in the after-school class. Rakib and Charlotte linked their teaching around topics such as healthy eating, and the children drew pictures of fruit and labelled them in Bengali for a display in the classroom.

Rakib had a clear vision of how to develop a multilingual approach across the curriculum, drawing on his experience as a mainstream teacher who had also run the Bengali after-school class for many years. He believed children should be able to develop academic language in their mother tongue alongside English through the mainstream curriculum. Then, for example, children learning Bengali as well as English would become proficient in both languages and would be able to work in both Bangladesh and the UK. Rakib knew the benefits of exploring a topic in more than one language to maximise children's understanding. To facilitate cross-curricular multilingual learning, he regularly liaised with the French language teacher as well as class teachers. So the topic of the rainforest was addressed in English in the general primary curriculum, in Bengali and French in the respective language lessons, and in Bengali in the after-school complementary class. Each teacher covered related content in a variety of ways: the children created a colourful display about rainforest animals in English and Bengali, and they roleplayed different animals in the forest while singing a French song. This was the kind of approach we hoped to explore further through the research project.

However, Rakib considered that the current curriculum, particularly in upper primary years, did not encourage multicultural work, focusing as it did on topics such as the Vikings, Romans and Victorians in ways that offered little obvious connection with countries such as Bangladesh. The new International Primary Curriculum was more flexible, and he envisaged studying a topic such as how food is grown in different countries. The children could investigate this by talking with parents at home. They would discover a rich variety of words in Bengali for different stages of rice growing, so they could understand this process in depth. They could learn about each other's languages; Rakib found that when teaching Bengali in mainstream class, non-Bengali speaking pupils, too, often showed great interest and learnt quickly.

The mainstream teachers were therefore keen to form partnerships with complementary teachers and change a situation in which, as Charlotte said, 'we're really operating as two very separate entities at the moment'. Shah, from Bengali Community School, made a similar point:

> We are working in two different parts and we are supporting each other, here only my head is working, and I teach here and when there are two heads here there will be more to learn and everything will come forward ... ideas, discussions...

Shah highlighted the fact that complementary and mainstream schools were teaching the same pupils, but the connections were not yet being exploited. It was interesting to see how children responded when teachers began to visit each other's settings and link up their curricula.

Making the connections

The children were surprised and delighted when they saw their mainstream teachers arrive at their complementary school or vice versa. Some found it hard to believe at first. When we told a child that his Russian complementary school teacher and his primary teacher would be working together, he could not imagine how the two schools could be joined up: 'Are you going to knock down my primary school, or build a tunnel?' His response indicated that until now he had experienced the separation as inevitable.

When her mainstream teacher Alison visited her Bengali class, another child commented that: 'it was the first time someone came from school to see us'. Alison's pupils were thrilled when she came to a talent show at Bengali school and would not let her leave until she had seen them perform. Pupils in Somali class welcomed James enthusiastically and included his name in sentences they were writing in Somali. And when Annika visited Bengali complementary school, Sumaya made a bilingual game for her that bridged the two settings. She folded a sheet of paper so that the outer layer showed Bengali numbers. When Annika selected each number, the paper opened out to reveal a different message in English.

At primary school, the Bengali teachers were immediately surrounded by excited children in the playground. Some of the children were their own pupils, whilst others recognised them as teachers because of their Islamic dress and began talking about the Bengali or Arabic classes they attended. The headteacher of one of the Bengali schools was astonished when so many of his pupils ran up to him, exclaiming 'this is my school, all my children are here'. When Bengali complementary teachers visited primary classrooms, pupils vied with each other to be the one to escort them and greeted them with *asalaam aleikum*. Rapport was quickly established. Children in Hamida's nursery class, for example, began asking their visitor Redwan about his family. As Alison said, 'I know the children were really pleased to see me there [in Bengali school] and really thrilled to see Mr Shah in this school as well'.

The children from Somali or Russian backgrounds were in a linguistic minority at primary school, and when their complementary teachers first appeared there they had more complex reactions. Being different from others was difficult in itself in a monolingual institution where children's languages and cultures were not recognised in the curriculum. If you were of Bangladeshi origin you were at least part of the majority ethnic group in the school, even though your language had less status than English. The teachers had already told us that children from other backgrounds felt their difference more acutely and were sometimes excluded by their classmates. Having a teacher there who spoke their language was particularly important for giving these children support, but speaking with that teacher in Somali or Russian also highlighted their minority position, so it took time for them to feel secure about using their home languages. As they did so, however, their self-confidence grew noticeably.

When two Somali children were chosen to escort complementary teacher Osman around their primary school, they were at first embarrassed about speaking Somali with him. They gradually became more involved in conversation while they were showing him mosaic sculptures they had made. After that they felt confident enough to invite Osman to visit their class and they asked him to sit with them as they worked. Natasha from the Russian school described as 'priceless' the expression on the faces of her pupils when she arrived at their primary school: 'They read just one question: 'What are you doing here?'' One child seemed uncomfortable when she first spoke Russian to him in the classroom, but he later exuded confidence after leading his classmates in acting out a Russian story as part of the research project.

Cultural knowledge and family links

Through visiting the complementary schools, the mainstream teachers gained deeper understanding of the cultural learning that took place there. Alison witnessed children reading Bengali poetry and talked with them about the beautiful language used by the famous writer, Tagore. As well as literary language, children were learning about moral values, for example through Islamic stories that often parallel those in the Bible. Hamida observed Redwan telling his Bengali class the story of Sulaman (Solomon) giving judgement in the case of the two women who both claimed to be the mother of the same baby, and eliciting from the children the moral 'A real mother won't harm her baby'.

The mainstream teachers came to realise that complementary schools helped children recover the cultural knowledge they had lost due to growing up in a new country. When James first visited Zainab's Somali class, parents and children arranged a display of cultural artefacts from Somalia and performed Somali songs and dances for him. Children eagerly volunteered to name each item and explain its use, but some of them did not know about these artefacts and only learned what they were during the session. Parents and Somali teachers emphasised how important it was to build the children's knowledge so they could feel confident when visiting Somalia and eventually pass on their heritage to the next generation.

All complementary schools evidently had strong links with families. Primary teachers attending the annual celebration at a Bengali school were impressed by the number of grandparents, parents, teenagers and babies who were crammed into the room as the audience. The Russian school was preparing special celebrations for Mother's Day, to which parents would be invited. In Zainab's Somali class, the parents were participants. Sitting at the back, they called out reminders to children who were misbehaving. They supported learning by making suggestions in Somali, and children would run over to them for help. James remarked that the class reminded him of a student-run study group he had joined at university, where members collaborated to facilitate understanding. He recognised that the class operated as a learning community in which parents were directly involved.

As partners in the research project, the complementary and mainstream teachers devised lessons drawing on children's linguistic and cultural knowledge, and involving their families. Topics included stories and poems in different languages which had parallel themes, jobs in different countries, learning about plants through gardening with parents, learning about fruit and vegetables grown in different countries, bread-making with parents, and the names of the animals in the Noah's Ark story – linking the Islamic and Christian versions. We focus here on three examples of partnership work in the second year of the research.

At this point the complementary teachers were invited to join mainstream colleagues in School A at planning meetings to prepare topics for the new International Primary Curriculum. The first example concerns the topic of Grandparents, and shows the complementary teacher's awareness of how to help children develop intergenerational relationships in families dislocated by migration. In the second example, The Rag Trade, the complementary teacher drew on his own life history to introduce children to the complex issue of global trading, linking their lives in London with those of child labourers in Bangladesh. The final example, Living Together, demonstrated how the complementary teacher's holistic approach helped children understand abstract concepts such as interdependence and community. In each case, the complementary teacher's expertise supported mainstream colleagues to develop a curriculum that interconnected with home and community experience and enriched children's learning.

Grandparents: connecting with families

The research project aimed to help parents and grandparents participate in children's learning, and teacher partners were encouraged to consider this in their planning. Annika recognised that grandparents played a key part in children's lives, and in her initial interview she had reflected on the importance of learning with her Swedish grandmother. She suggested that as part of the International Primary Curriculum topic for 5-7 year olds, Our World, children could investigate the places where their grandparents lived.

Osman, who taught the Somali after-school class at the primary school, was working on the topic with Annika and colleagues. He knew from his own experience that children needed to strengthen relationships with grandparents when families had migrated, because there was often a linguistic and cultural gap between the generations. In the case of Somali families, most grandparents were not even in the UK, as they were separated by war. Osman had noticed that some of his pupils did not know key vocabulary for family members. One wanted to address him as 'uncle', a term children would use to their teacher, but called him 'aunt' instead, not realising it was incorrect. They also did not know the appropriate expressions in Somali to relate respectfully to adults.

Osman suggested a family tree picture as a starting point to help children explore their roots and learn more about their home language. He drew a *qudhac* or acacia, a tree that is significant in the desert environment of Somalia. Each child could write their own name on the trunk of the tree. On the lower branches Osman wrote terms for siblings in Somali and English, and on the higher ones words for parents and grandparents (see Figure 11). In Somali class the children acted out their family tree, starting from *aniga* (me), then stepping forward and gesturing to either side as they said *waba-*

Figure 11: Family tree in Somali

shay (sister) and *walaalkay* (brother), naming their siblings as they did so, and stepping forward again to name the next generation. In this way they developed a sense of being physically connected with their family members.

The children arrived at the following class excitedly clutching photos of grandparents. The pictures were battered with use and evidently well-loved. Osman helped the children prepare to talk to their grandparents on the phone or write to them, by roleplaying conversations through which they learnt how to address an older person appropriately. The children and parents then worked together on a powerpoint presentation showing photos of grandparents alongside messages in Somali with English translation (see Figure 12 overleaf for an example). They proudly presented their work to a whole-school assembly at school, at which Somali was used for the first time, and again to an audience of 500 people at the Tower Hamlets Languages Celebration.

Annika and her primary school colleagues organised a Grandparents Afternoon, and were delighted by the number of grandparents and parents from different cultural backgrounds who arrived, many of whom had never visited the school before. Waving to their family members in the audience, the children showed topic work they had produced in class, including drawings of their grandparents and pieces of writing about what they enjoyed doing together. The grandparents translated Osman's family tree diagram into other languages and discussed similarities and differences between the words they used. Finally, the grandparents visited classes for a question and answer session with the children about their lives.

This work made the grandparents feel the school valued their cultural background and their contribution to the children's learning. Children strengthened relationships with grandparents near and far, linking with their family heritage to develop their multilingual identities and build confidence as learners. Osman produced new curriculum work which met the needs of his complementary class, leading the way for primary teachers to explore the topic at a deeper and more personal level with children from different backgrounds.

The Rag Trade: connecting across countries
Teachers of Years 5 and 6 initially thought the topic Global Swapshop, concerning international trade, would be rather difficult for their 10-11 year old pupils. But their Bengali teacher partner Shah immediately saw the relevance to children's lives. Children could check the labels in their clothes to see where they had been made and discuss the prices that had been paid for them.

My sweet grandma I miss you
could you come with me
bye bye.
Rahima

AYEEYO LUUL

Rahima

Asalaamu caleykum

Ayeeyo macan wanku xisay ii imow.

Nabadeey ayeeyo luul.

Figure 12: Rahima's message to her grandmother

Clothes bought cheaply in the high street often came from countries such as Bangladesh, where child labour still existed. Shah pointed out that many children's parents would have worked in the rag trade in East London too, generally in sweatshops or as homeworkers. He himself had worked in the Burberry factory, only to be made redundant when it was transferred to Bangladesh where labour was cheaper.

The primary teachers invited Shah to be interviewed by their classes. Shah went further by bringing a powerpoint presentation to stimulate the children's thinking about interconnections between their lives and those of children in other countries. He juxtaposed pictures of high street shops with photos of child labour, around a central picture of children in a UK primary school classroom. Shah used this presentation to generate discussion in the primary school and also in his Bengali complementary class. He provided keywords in Bengali and English such as *shujuger bebohar* (exploit), *bebsha* (trade), *srom* (labour) and *sromer mullo* (Fair Trade). One photo showed workers protesting in Bangladesh, holding placards with slogans in Bengali and the words 'Save Our Life' in English. The children worked out the meaning of the Bengali text, helped in primary school by a pupil who had built up good literacy skills in Bengali after-school class. Shah suggested that the children could also interview their parents about their working lives in London and elsewhere, and he offered examples of possible questions for them to ask in Bengali and English. The primary school teachers built on this initiative through an activity in which the children wrote letters to tea companies as part of an international campaign for Fair Trade tea.

When Annika – a teacher at School A – visited Bangladesh with a teachers' delegation from Tower Hamlets, she took questions from pupils at her school and Shah's Bengali class to ask the children she met at a primary school there and at a night school for child workers. Based on the information she brought back, primary and complementary classes produced a joint presentation for Tower Hamlets Languages Celebration (see Figure 13 overleaf for an extract) in which they roleplayed interviews with children in Bangladesh. The young actors became intensely involved in their roles, bringing in shabby, torn clothes to wear as the factory worker characters. One child made an iron from cardboard covered in foil and brought a small ironing board along. The presentation finished with slogans the children had devised. These showed their empathy for their peers in Bangladesh, as well as their developing understanding of the global economy and the need for social justice. They read: 'Keep Child Labour Out Of The World!' and 'Each Child Deserves A Life Of Their Own!'.

Child's Question from Bangladesh

Do children in England have to work?

Answer: No, we are not allowed to work. We are very lucky

না , আমাদের এখানে কাজ করার নিয়ম নাই। আমরা খুব ভাগ্যবান।

(Na, ammader ekhane kaj korar niom nai. Amora khube bhaggoban)

Figure 13: Extract from Rag Trade presentation

Shah was able to lead on this topic because he had such a comprehensive knowledge of the children's everyday lives in London, their parents' life histories, and links to their countries of origin. His own experience had also given him a sharp understanding of the sociopolitical issues involved in global trade. A child who took part in the work at both her schools, complementary and primary, commented 'I didn't know all this before and my Bengali teacher made a difference because he's from Bangladesh and he taught us a lot about it'. Shah's partnership with mainstream colleagues enhanced the pupils' learning by bringing challenging issues into the curriculum and helping children reflect critically on the interconnections.

Living Together: connecting communities

The complementary teachers brought a holistic perspective to their work, as demonstrated by Sulaman, headteacher at Bengali Community School, when he taught the topic Living Together in partnership with Year 3 and 4 teachers at primary school. Like Osman, Sulaman used the metaphor of a tree, this time to represent a community rather than a family. He drew a detailed picture of a jackfruit tree, which is common in Bangladesh, with roots, branches and fruit. He explained that the tree could symbolise a society, such as London or the UK, with roots in different countries joining in the trunk to make one tree. The branches could be communities from different cultural backgrounds, bearing fruit if they are living together in harmony. The tree could also be a school community with pupils from different backgrounds as the branches, or it could be a child who might have roots in different countries and languages. A society is enriched by different individuals and communities, just as an orchard or garden is enriched by having a variety of trees.

Sulaman helped plan lessons in which the children first drew their own tree and considered why trees are important to our environment: giving shade, producing oxygen and taking in carbon dioxide, and creating fruit and seed for new trees. This showed them that trees are essential to life, so we need to plant seeds and look after them by adding compost, watering and protecting them. The class then discussed how a school community can grow and develop like a tree, if children from different backgrounds are working well together. The topic was taught successfully by Sulaman with his Bengali class at complementary school, and by Rakib in primary school for cross-curricular work in Bengali lessons.

In primary school, Year 4 children produced trees representing the variety of languages in their class, with roots labelled 'Somali', 'Urdu', 'Bengali', 'Turkish', 'Swedish', 'Dutch' and 'Hindi' and also 'English', (see Figure 14). The tree con-

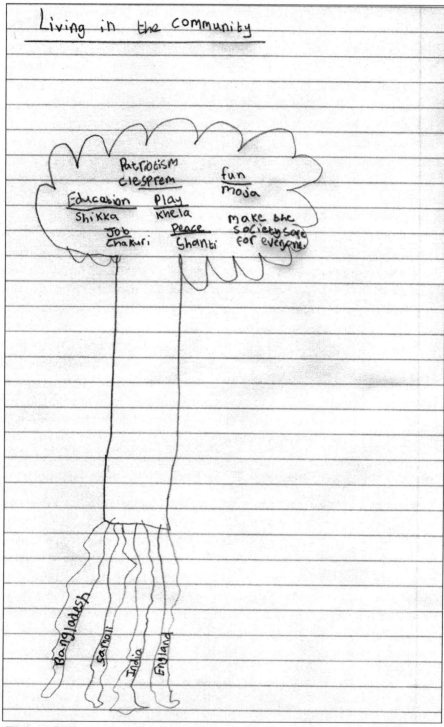

Figure 14: Zaid's tree representing roots of his class and values for the school community

cept was flexible, enabling children to include different aspects of their multilingual identities, as speakers of English as well as other languages. They talked with Rakib about what was important to create a community and came up with ideas such as *shanti*/peace, *shikka*/education and *khela*/play, which they wrote amongst the leaves of their trees.

Sulaman's next step in the Living Together topic was to compare village life to city life in Bangladesh, using photos as a springboard for ideas. One picture showed a typical village courtyard in Bangladesh, surrounded by houses each belonging to a different family. Sulaman devised questions to encourage the children to consider how everyone in the village worked together, each family growing different crops and sharing their produce and income. A photo of a busy city street in Bangladesh with high-rise buildings facilitated a discussion about how families function in a city, and how each member makes an individual contribution to their own family group. Thus Sulaman's approach covered not only the practical aspects of food or jobs but also the network of human relationships that helped a community to function. The questions could be taken home to parents to ask about village or city life in different countries, and also used to make comparisons with rural and urban life in the UK.

Sulaman often taught Bengali literacy through his own poetry, and for this topic he composed a poem in Bengali about 'My Village', describing the natural environment of a Bangladeshi village and its sense of community. He wrote a contrasting poem about 'The City', evoking the noise and bustle of city life. He then taught a lesson comparing the two poems with Year 4 children in primary school and also in his own Bengali class. The children enjoyed hearing the poem in Bengali and finding out the translation in English, and it inspired them to talk about their own experiences of visiting rural areas or cities beyond the UK.

This holistic approach helped the children understand complex International Primary Curriculum learning targets such as 'how independence and interdependence are important when people live together in communities'. Sulaman's visual metaphor of 'community as a tree' generated many possible meanings that children could apply to their own lives, providing support for their abstract thinking.

Children's agency as learners

As the curriculum opened out at primary school, children demonstrated linguistic and cultural knowledge previously hidden from their teachers. The children who had initially been embarrassed to speak Somali with Osman came forward to share their language when James asked them to help teach the class a Somali song. Abdilahi, who had often been difficult in class, sat at the edge of the group at first. As he saw the enthusiasm expressed by his teacher and classmates, Abdilahi gradually moved across the floor until he was at James' feet. He then climbed up on a bench to act as teacher.

Since the project work was multilingual, it promoted all the children's languages within each primary school class. A child in Siobhan's class was known to speak Pashto, but it turned out he could speak three other languages too and was literate in Farsi. Alison commented on the effect of bringing in dual language storybooks: 'the biggest thing was seeing the impact of children using their mother tongue language within the classroom, the effect it had on their self-esteem was so high'. A child struggling with English literacy turned out to be a fluent reader in Turkish. After sharing a dual language storybook with the whole class, he was surrounded in the playground by children wanting to learn Turkish words. Another child who 'doesn't really have much of a voice' became confident for the first time when reading in Urdu. A child who 'hardly ever spoke in English' to Alison 'suddenly actually wanted to use her mother tongue, wanting to bring books and talk in Somali ... that's really developed my relationship with her'.

Children could draw on a greater range of knowledge because the topic work related to their home and community experiences. Four-year-olds in Hamida's nursery class vividly described their memories of Bangladesh: 'it rains there and the mud is always soggy'. In Jane's nursery class, children helping a Somali parent to mix dough started talking about making different kinds of bread at home. Children whose complementary and mainstream education had previously been kept separate could now link up their learning. After working on a Russian story with her primary school partner Jo, Natasha remarked that: 'The children were completely immersed in their work on the story for a week at both schools in both languages ... they finally saw a connection between their day-to-day activities and Russian school'.

Validating children's languages in mainstream school promoted their learner identities in complementary school as well. Sasha, the Russian child who had tried to picture how his two schools could be connected, was initially inattentive in primary school and shy in complementary school. He became more confident and focused in both settings after leading a performance in Russian in his primary school class. Natasha reported that 'He has changed now that I've seen him in his English school ... now he helps me in Russian school and tells me stories of what he did in the week ... he really enjoys learning Russian and thinks it is something 'cool'.'

Increasing family participation

The mainstream teachers began to take new steps to link with families, reaching out to parents and grandparents for help with topic work. Siobhan invited parents into her Year 6 class to be interviewed about the topic Memories of School. An Afghani mother came into school for the first time ever to take part in the parent panel, answering questions from children with her son as interpreter. Shaheen explained how she asked parents for suggestions about different topics: 'You have to search for these ideas – now I go to the parents, ask the parents. They are over the moon to be consulted'.

The Grandparents Afternoon widened participation for families whose first language was English as well as for bilingual families. A grandmother born and brought up in the East End was delighted to join in with the family tree activity, writing the different names that her UK-based and US-based grandchildren used for her. Her daughter-in-law was Bangladeshi and she had three bilingual grandchildren at the school, with whose lives she was closely involved. She was keen to continue working with children in class to share her life history in the local area. She said: 'I want to talk to them about things like coins, games we used to play, clothes we used to wear, oh so many things.'

The primary school was reaching out to parents on a more equal basis than before. When Annika returned from her visit to Bangladesh, she arranged a meeting in which she invited parents to share their experiences of education in different countries and discuss what they found positive or negative about schooling in England. Valuing parents' knowledge opened up two-way communication about approaches to learning. This mutual exchange went beyond the one-way transmission that typically takes place when parents are summoned to hear what happens in school.

Linking families across complementary and mainstream classes brought together parents from different language backgrounds. An after-school gardening session involved Rakib's after-school Bengali class, Osman's Somali class and Shaheen's Year 1 class. Children and parents mingled as they helped each other plant seedlings and water the pots. Shaheen noted how the activity promoted interaction between parents who usually kept to their own community group. During the project, parents at School A decided to start a parents' group. This was parent-led rather than school-initiated because, as a Somali parent explained, 'now parents really have respect for each other and we have a Parents' Group ... everyone needs each other'. Its success led to the setting up of a parent-teacher association through which parents of diverse origins could communicate with teachers and actively co-construct the school community.

Teachers creating a new curriculum

Mainstream teachers began to draw upon their own linguistic and cultural resources, inspired by the lead of their complementary teacher partners. Two class teachers in School A, both Bangladeshi, were working on the Living Together topic. They first intended to compare London with an English village, but after discussion with Sulaman they realised they could bring in children's knowledge of village life in Bangladesh or elsewhere. A group planning with Osman for a topic on Water included several teachers from a Muslim background. They suggested that children could talk about Islamic washing rituals before prayer, and make comparisons with observances in other faiths.

Shaheen, as class teacher, and Rakib, as Bengali teacher, were able to plan lessons together for the first time, pooling their bilingual and bicultural expertise. Shaheen was thrilled when Rakib introduced her to the Bengali font on the school's computer system, which she had not known about. For the topic on Bangladesh, they introduced Shaheen's class to Bengali songs from their own childhoods, demonstrating shared empathy as they sang together with the children. Shaheen began to talk about her memories of cooking with her grandmother as she and Rakib created worksheets on typical Bengali dishes. Similarly, Annika shared with her class a Swedish lullaby from her childhood, and they eagerly requested it the following day. The teachers' depth of engagement arose from drawing on personal experience, particularly multilingual experience. The standard monolingual and monocultural curriculum, with its narrow target-driven focus, had kept them disconnected from their own 'funds of knowledge' as well as those of their students. Now they could construct a new kind of curriculum that would make richer connections with a wider world.

It was striking to see how quickly the mainstream teachers involved in the project, whether from bilingual or monolingual backgrounds, adapted to planning for this new curriculum. Hamida found it straightforward to incorporate a lesson on jobs in different countries into her weekly plan for the topic Where People Work, and Annika built an entire week's literacy lessons around a comparison between Bengali and English poetry.

Siobhan was unsure how to plan for Memories of School at first, because 'it's not the type of lesson we usually do'. But after a discussion on the benefits of multilingual learning she decided on a number of objectives, including finding out about family history and building intercultural understanding, and her plan showed how the lesson would develop literacy skills too.

This research shows it is possible to devise a multilingual curriculum in mainstream school that links to children's home and community learning. Complementary teachers, families and children can help mainstream teachers see beyond the system that constrains them. This gives new meaning to the concept of partnership with parents and the community, because it is they who are taking the lead. When mainstream and complementary teachers combine their knowledge to jointly construct the curriculum, the *learning power* previously developed in community settings expands and grows stronger.

This process can only take place if knowledge from outside mainstream school is truly valued as a basis for learning. Mutual respect and equal support between the mainstream and complementary sectors are vital if children's worlds are to become truly interconnected in order to provide a firm foundation for learning across both settings. The teacher partnership project demonstrated the overall benefits of such collaboration. In Alison's words, 'It made the children see we're not separate entities in their lives and that we're all part and parcel of their education'.

Ideas for creating a multilingual curriculum

- When planning a topic, you could make a checklist of the following aspects:
  - How will you link the topic to students' cultural knowledge?
  - How will you involve the students' languages?
  - How will you involve parents and families?

  Complementary and mainstream teachers can brainstorm together and create a map of potential activities for each topic.

- If children work on a topic across their different sites of learning, this will reinforce and enhance their understanding of concepts, as in the example of studying The Rainforest in Bengali class, mainstream class and French lessons at mainstream school. This approach is similar to CLIL (Content and Language Integrated Learning) which is now being used successfully in schools in the UK and internationally.

- Resources and sample lesson plans for cross-curricular multilingual work developed by teachers on the research project are available on the Goldsmiths Multilingual Learning webpages at: http://www.gold. ac.uk/clcl/multilingual-learning/cmp/

The work on bilingual poetry, Grandparents, the Rag Trade and Living Together can be found here, as well as a number of other topics including stories and food from different cultures.

- Resources from a Goldsmiths research project by Jim Anderson and Yu-Chiao Chung on developing multilingual skills through arts-based creativity are at: http://www.gold.ac.uk/clcl/multilingual-learning/ creativity/

- Ideas for collaborative activities between mainstream and complementary schools developed from our research include:
  - jointly hosting an International Languages Celebration or Talent Show
  - holding a Bilingualism Advice Panel where parents work in groups to prepare questions for panel members who can include complementary teachers, speech and language therapists, researchers and parents raising bilingual children
  - dual-language book making sessions with parents in partnership with complementary teachers
  - a dual-language book library at school from which parents and complementary classes can regularly borrow

  Many other examples of collaboration from the UK-wide Our Languages project, such as mainstream schools offering premises for complementary classes and complementary teachers supporting educational achievement and parental involvement, can be found at: http://www.ourlanguages.org.uk

- The Model of Partnership presentation by one of the primary schools involved in our research shows examples of collaborative activities and sums up the benefits of linking with complementary schools. The presentation is available at: http://www.gold.ac.uk/media/ Model%20of%20Partnership.pps

  Here the school reflects on developing a more creative and relevant curriculum, developing children's collaborative learning skills and fostering partnership with parents – the rich harvest that comes from interconnecting children's worlds.

Conclusion:
Promoting Learning Power

Teachers need to take the lead in connecting children's worlds. At present, children themselves are the only points of connection. They are aware of their different experiences in community settings or mainstream school but are often required to keep their worlds artificially separate. Teachers have greater power and authority so they can take action for change, initiating processes through which children's agency as learners can grow.

Complementary teachers are ready to collaborate with their mainstream colleagues in this process. Many are already working across settings, combining a daytime role as teacher or teaching assistant with their after-school or weekend complementary class. Complementary teachers told us of their wish to make links with mainstream schools, and some described the efforts they had already made to do so. There are some excellent partnerships around the UK, many begun through the Our Languages project (Our Languages, 2012) and through local authority forums supported by the National Resource Centre for Supplementary Education (NRC, 2012).

All too often, however, when complementary headteachers approach their local mainstream schools, their phone calls are not returned. They are seen as unimportant and marginal in children's education. Yet this book has shown how central their contribution is, and how vital it is for mainstream teachers to understand and appreciate it. Home and community experiences underpin children's learning and it is crucial to bring their linguistic and cultural knowledge into the mainstream curriculum.

Mainstream schools can make a difference by actively reaching out to complementary schools to share resources and provide a forum for the exchange of expertise. Complementary schools are often battling against the odds in cramped spaces with few materials, yet they are developing innovative teaching strategies and involving families to create effective learning communities.

Mainstream schools can offer complementary schools free access to classrooms and new technology, make space available to display children's work, and invite complementary teachers to join in-service training sessions where they can share ideas with mainstream colleagues.

The rewards are impressive. The children's learning is taken further by both the schools they attend. Complementary schools benefit from better resources and support for teacher development. Meanwhile, complementary classes and cultural activities are made available to pupils at the mainstream school. Mainstream schools benefit from greater parental involvement and can consult complementary teachers on how to help their students to progress. Recent UK research has found convincing evidence that children who attend complementary schools do better in the mainstream than bilingual children who do not (Evans and Vassie, 2012).

Through visiting complementary classes and working in partnership with colleagues there, mainstream teachers can better understand how to build learning communities in their own classrooms. At present, teachers have only partial knowledge of their bilingual pupils, since these children present only certain aspects of their identities in mainstream school. In order to fit in with the monolingual and monocultural ethos of the curriculum, they suppress many of the linguistic and cultural competences they possess. In addition, the target-driven mainstream system promotes a competitive individualistic approach in which children are continually classified and ranked, and low expectations are usually held of those who have bilingual backgrounds.

Often mainstream teachers only realise the potential talents of their pupils when they see what happens in complementary schools. Children who seem to be low achievers or to have learning difficulties may operate very differently when they can use all their language resources and participate in a mutually supportive group. Even high-achieving children may be working to less than their full capacity in mainstream school, when they could enhance their learning bilingually and gain extra confidence as they begin to feel more secure in their multiple cultural identities. A curriculum that draws on home and community knowledge and involves families is one important step in making change. Creating a learning community in the classroom is another. The two aspects are integrally connected; neither will work without the other.

Teachers often feel they do not have time to engage with change. They are driven to distraction by the demands of government initiatives, inspections and form-filling, none of which leaves space for independent thought or collective action. However, time spent working collaboratively with complementary teachers, children and families will be amply rewarded, building long-term partnerships for learning. The children's self-esteem rises rapidly. The home and community support they receive multiplies the number of people involved in their education. Consequently, teachers' time is actually saved and the children's achievement is higher.

Some teachers feel worried that if they encourage the use of different languages, this will undermine their control in the classroom. How will they understand what is happening, or assess children's learning? This is where it is important to understand the nature of *learning power*. Earlier we defined this as 'working together as a community, co-constructing knowledge that draws on multilingual and multicultural resources'. If children share their language expertise and cultural experiences, they will become teachers as well as learners. They will actively participate in classroom strategies and in the curriculum, taking responsibility for others' learning as well as their own. Teachers will see how working bilingually improves the thinking and writing children produce in English, and how parents and complementary teachers can be involved as part of the learning community.

For children, *learning power* means both the power to learn, and learning to use that power. Linking their community and mainstream lives will increase their sense of agency and engage them fully with the process of learning. For teachers, *learning power* is built by collaborating with mainstream or complementary colleagues, as well as with children and families. In mainstream schools, this means teachers will no longer feel, as one of our participants said, that 'there's always that little bit that's missing' in their relationships with children from different linguistic and cultural backgrounds. Instead, teachers can relate to the whole child. Through interconnecting worlds, education becomes a shared creative activity in which teachers and children move forward in learning together.

References

Ajegbo, K (2007) *Curriculum Review: diversity and citizenship.* London, HMSO

Al-Azami, S, Kenner, C, Ruby, M and Gregory, E (2010) Transliteration as a bridge to learning for bilingual children. *International Journal of Bilingual Education and Bilingualism* 13(6) p683-700

Anderson, J (2008) Pre- and in-service professional development of teachers of community/ heritage languages in the UK: insider perspectives. *Language, Culture and Curriculum 22 (4) p283-297*

Anderson, J, Kenner, C and Gregory, E (2008) The National Languages Strategy in the UK: are minority languages still on the margins? In Helot, C and de Mejia, A (eds) *Forging Multilingual Spaces: integrated perspectives on majority and minority bilingual education.* Clevedon: Multilingual Matters

Anderson, J and Chung, Y-C (2011) Finding a voice: arts-based creativity in the community languages classroom. *International Journal of Bilingual Education and Bilingualism* 14 (5) p551-569

Barnhardt, R and Kawagley, O (2005) Indigenous knowledge systems and Alaska native ways of knowing. *Anthropology and Education Quarterly* 36 (1) p8-23

Barradas, O and Chen, Y (2008) How Portuguese and Chinese community schools support educational achievement. In Kenner, C and Hickey, T (eds)

Blackledge, A and Creese, A (2010) *Multilingualism: a critical perspective.* London: Continuum

Botelho, M, Cohen, S, Leoni, L, Chow, P and Sastri, P (2009) Respecting children's cultural and linguistic knowledge: the pedagogical possibilities and challenges of multiliteracies in schools. In Dantas, M and Manyak, P (eds)

Bourdieu, P (1991) *Language and Symbolic Power.* Cambridge: Polity Press

Brinton, D, Kagan, O and Bauckus, S (eds) (2008) *Heritage Language Education: a new field emerging.* New York: Routledge

Causley, C (1975) *Collected Poems 1951-1975.* London: Macmillan

Chen, Y and Gregory, E (2004) 'How do I read these words?': bilingual exchange teaching between Cantonese-speaking peers. In Gregory, E, Long, S and Volk, D (eds) *Many Pathways to Literacy: young children learning with siblings, grandparents, peers and communities.* London: Routledge Falmer

Clyne, M and Fernandez, S (2008) Community language learning in Australia. *Encyclopedia of Language Education (2nd edition) 4, Second and Foreign Language Education.* New York: Springer

Collaborative Learning (2012) http://www.collaborativelearning.org/wordymaths.pdf (accessed July 2012)

Conteh, J (2010) Making links across complementary and mainstream classrooms for primary children and their teachers. In Lytra, V and Martin, P (eds)

Conteh, J and Begum, S (2008) Bilingual teachers as agents of social change: linking the community and the mainstream. In Kenner, C and Hickey, T (eds)

Conteh, J and Brock, A (2011) 'Safe spaces'? Sites of bilingualism for young learners in home, school and community. *International Journal of Bilingual Education and Bilingualism* 14 (3) p347-360

Crawford, J (2000) *At War with Diversity: US language policy in an age of anxiety*. Clevedon, Avon: Multilingual Matters

Creese, A, Bhatt, A, Bhojani, N and Martin, P (2006) Multicultural, heritage and learner identities in complementary schools. *Language and Education* 20 (1) p23-43

Cruickshank, K (2004) Literacy in multilingual contexts: change in teenagers' reading and writing. *Language and Education* 18 (6) p459-473

Cummins, J (2001) *Negotiating Identities: education for empowerment in a diverse society. 2nd ed.* Ontario, CA: California Association for Bilingual Education

Cummins, J (2005) A proposal for action: strategies for recognizing heritage language competence as a learning resource within the mainstream classroom. *The Modern Language Journal* 89 (4) p585-592

Cummins, J (2010) Spaced out: expanding interpersonal spaces for language learning through bilingual instructional strategies. Plenary address at the conference Plurilingual and Pluricultural Education: Focus on Languages of the Wider World. SOAS, London, 20 February

Cummins, J and Early, M (eds) (2011) *Identity Texts: the collaborative creation of power in multilingual schools*. Stoke-on-Trent: Trentham Books

Curdt-Christiansen, X-L (2006) Teaching and learning Chinese: heritage language classroom discourse in Montreal. *Language, Culture and Curriculum* 19 (2) p189-207

Dantas, M and Manyak, P (eds) (2009) *Home-School Connections in a Multicultural Society: learning from and with culturally and linguistically diverse families*. London: Routledge

Dash, P (2010) *African Caribbean Pupils in Art Education*. Rotterdam: Sense Publishers

Datta, M (2007) *Bilinguality and Literacy: principles and practice (2nd edition)*. London: Continuum

DES (1985) *Education for All. Report of the Committee of Inquiry into the Education of Ethnic Minority Groups. The Swann Report*. London: HMSO

DfES (2003) *Aiming High: raising the achievement of minority ethnic pupils*. Annesley, Notts: DfES

DfES (2006) *Excellence and Enjoyment: learning and teaching for bilingual children in the primary years*. Professional development materials. Norwich: OPSI

Duff, P (2008) Heritage language education in Canada. In Brinton, D., Kagan, O. and Bauckus, S. (eds)

Edwards, V, Monaghan, F and Knight, J (2000) Books, pictures and conversations: using bilingual multimedia storybooks to develop language awareness. *Language Awareness* 9 (3) p135-146

Eilers, R, Pearson, B and Cobo-Lewis, A (2006) Social factors in bilingual development: the Miami experience. In McCardle, P and Hoff, E (eds) *Childhood Bilingualism: research on infancy through school age*. Clevedon: Multilingual Matters

Evans, D and Vassie, P (2012) *Report Evidencing the Impact of Supplementary Education Across the Beneficial Area of John Lyon's Charity.* http://www.johnlyonscharity.org.uk/initiatives/schools/documents/Supplementary_School_Impact_Report_June2012.pdf (accessed July 2012)

Foucault, M (1980) *Power/Knowledge: selected interviews and other writings 1972-1977*. London: Harvester Press

Francis, B, Archer, L and Mau, A (2010) Chinese complementary school pupils' social and educational subjectivities. In Lytra, V. and Martin, P. (eds)

Gillborn, D (2005) Education policy as an act of white supremacy: whiteness, critical race theory and education reform. *Journal of Education Policy* 20 (4) p485-505

Glynn, T and Berryman, M (2003) A community elder's role in improving reading and writing for Māori students. In Barnard, R and Glynn, T (eds) *Bilingual Children's Language and Literacy Development*. Clevedon: Multilingual Matters

Gregory, E (2001) Sisters and brothers as language and literacy teachers: synergy between siblings playing and working together. *Journal of Early Childhood Literacy* 1(3) p301-322

Gregory, E and Williams, A (2000) *City Literacies*. London: Routledge

Gregory, E, Long, S and Volk, D (2004) A sociocultural approach to learning. In Gregory, E, Long, S and Volk, D (eds) *Many Pathways to Literacy*. London: Routledge

Gregory, E, Arju, T, Jessel, J, Kenner, C and Ruby, M (2007) Snow White in different guises: interlingual and intercultural exchanges between grandparents and young children at home in East London. *Journal of Early Childhood Literacy* 7 (1) p5-25

Gregory, E, Choudhury, H, Ilankuberan, A, Kwapong, A and Woodham, M (forthcoming) Practise, performance and perfection: learning sacred texts in four faith communities in London. *International Journal of the Sociology of Language in Education*

Hall, K, Özerk. K, Zulfiqar, M and Tan, J (2002) 'This is our school': provision, purpose and pedagogy of supplementary schooling in Leeds and Oslo. *British Educational Research Journal* 28 (3) p399-418

Heller, M (1995) Language choice, social institutions, and symbolic domination. *Language in Society* 24, p373-405

Hornberger, N and Wang, S (2008) Who are our heritage language learners? Identity and biliteracy in heritage language education in the United States. In Brinton, D, Kagan, O and Bauckus, S (eds)

Issa, T and Williams, C (2009) *Realising Potential: complementary schools in the UK*. Stoke-on-Trent: Trentham Books

Kenner, C (2000) *Home Pages: literacy links for bilingual children*. Stoke-on-Trent: Trentham Books

Kenner, C (2004a) *Becoming Biliterate: young children learning different writing systems*. Stoke-on-Trent: Trentham Books

Kenner, C (2004b) Living in simultaneous worlds: difference and integration in bilingual script-learning. *International Journal of Bilingual Education and Bilingualism* 7 (1) p43-61

Kenner, C (2005) Bilingual families as literacy eco-systems. *Early Years* 25 (3), p283-298

Kenner, C, Ruby, M, Gregory, E, Jessel, J and Arju, T (2007) Intergenerational learning between children and grandparents in East London. *Journal of Early Childhood Research* 5 (2) p219-243

Kenner, C, Al-Azami, S, Gregory, E and Ruby, M (2008a) Bilingual poetry: expanding the cognitive and cultural dimensions of children's learning. *Literacy* 42(2) p92-100

Kenner, C, Gregory, E, Ruby, M and Al-Azami, S (2008b) Bilingual learning for second and third generation children. *Language, Culture and Curriculum* 21 (2) p120-137

Kenner, C and Hickey, T (eds) (2008) *Multilingual Europe: diversity and learning*. Stoke-on-Trent: Trentham Books

Lam, E and Rosario-Ramos, E (2009) Multilingual literacies in transnational digitally mediated contexts: an exploratory study of immigrant teens in the United States. *Language and Education* 23 (2) p171-190

Lee, S and Hawkins, M (2008) 'Family is here': learning in community-based after-school programs. *Theory into Practice* 47 (1) p51-58

Lemberger, N (2002) Russian bilingual science learning: perspectives from secondary students. *International Journal of Bilingual Education and Bilingualism* 5 (1) p58-71

Liu, P (2006) Community-based Chinese schools in Southern California: a survey of teachers. *Language, Culture and Curriculum* 19(2) p237-247

Lo Bianco, J (2008) Policy activity for heritage languages: connections with representation and citizenship. In Brinton, D, Kagan, O and Bauckus, S (eds)

Long, S and Volk, D (2009) Networks of support: Learning from the other teachers in children's lives. In Dantas, M. and Manyak, P. (eds)

Lytra, V and Martin, P (eds) (2010) *Sites of Multilingualism: complementary schools in Britain today.* Stoke-on-Trent: Trentham Books

Martin, P, Bhatt, A, Bhojani, N and Creese, A (2007) Multilingual learning stories in two Gujarati complementary schools in Leicester. In Conteh, J, Martin, P and Helavaara Robertson, L (eds) *Multilingual Learning: stories from schools and communities in Britain.* Stoke-on-Trent: Trentham Books

Martin-Jones, M and Saxena, M (2003) Bilingual resources and 'funds of knowledge' for teaching and learning in multi-ethnic classrooms in Britain. *International Journal of Bilingual Education and Bilingualism* 6 (3) p267-282

May, S (ed) (1999) *Critical Multiculturalism: rethinking multicultural and antiracist education.* London: Falmer Press

Maylor, U, Glass, K, Issa, T, Kuyok, A, Minty, S, Rose, A and Ross, A (2010) *Impact of Supplementary Schools on Pupils' Attainment: an investigation into what factors contribute to educational improvements.* London: DCSF

Moll, L, Amanti, C, Neff, D and González, N (1992) Funds of knowledge for teaching; using a qualitative approach to connect homes and classrooms. *Theory into Practice* 31 (2) p132-141

Moore, D (2002) Case study: code-switching and learning in the classroom. *International Journal of Bilingual Education and Bilingualism* 5 (5) p279-293

NALDIC (2012a) http://www.naldic.org.uk/eal-teaching-and-learning/links (accessed July 2012)

NALDIC (2012b) http://www.naldic.org.uk/eal-teaching-and-learning/outline-guidance (accessed July 2012)

NRC (2012) http://www.continyou.org.uk/what_we_do/supplementary_education/ (accessed July 2012)

Nieto, S and Bode, P (2008) *Affirming Diversity: the sociopolitical context of multicultural education.* Boston: Allyn and Bacon

O'Rourke, B (2011) Negotiating multilingualism in an Irish primary school context. In Hélot, C and Ó Laoire, M (eds) *Language Policy for the Multilingual Classroom: pedagogy of the possible.* Cleveland, Avon: Multilingual Matters

Our Languages (2012) www.ourlanguages.org.uk (accessed July 2012)

Pantazi, E (2010) Teachers' developing theories and practices in Greek community schools. In Lytra, V and Martin, P (eds)

Pearce, S (forthcoming) Confronting dominant Whiteness in the primary classroom: Progressive student teachers' dilemmas and constraints. *Oxford Review of Education*

Robertson, L (2010) Developing links between communities, schools and initial teacher training. In Lytra, V and Martin, P (eds)

Robertson, L, Drury, R and Cable, C (under review) Silencing bilingualism. *International Journal of Early Years Education*

Rogoff, B (2003) *The Cultural Nature of Human Development.* New York: Oxford University Press

Rosowsky, A (2006) 'I used to copy what the teachers at school would do'. Cross-cultural fusion: the role of older children in community literacy practices. *Language and Education* 20 (6) p529-542

Ruby, M, Kenner, C, Jessel, J, Gregory, E and Arju, T (2007) Gardening with grandparents: an early engagement with the science curriculum. *Early Years* 27 (2) p131-144

Ruby, M, Gregory, E, Kenner, C and Al-Azami, S (2010) Grandmothers as orchestrators of early language and literacy lessons. In Lytra, V and Martin, P (eds)

Sneddon, R (2009) *Bilingual Books – Biliterate Children: learning to read through dual-language books*. Stoke-on-Trent: Trentham Books

Tran, A (2008) Vietnamese language education in the United States. *Language, Culture and Curriculum* 21 (3) p256-268

Tuafuti, P, and McCaffery, J (2005) Family and community empowerment through bilingual education. *International Journal of Bilingual Education and Bilingualism* 8 (5) p480-503

Valdés, G, González, S, López García, D and Márquez, P (2008) Heritage languages and ideologies of language: unexamined challenges. In Brinton, D, Kagan, O and Bauckus, S (eds)

Volk, D and De Acosta, M (2001) Many differing ladders, many ways to climb: literacy events in the bilingual classrooms, homes and community of three Puerto Rican kindergartners. *Journal of Early Childhood Literacy* 1 (2) p193-224

Vygotsky, L (1962) *Thought and Language*. Cambridge, Mass: MIT Press

Vygotsky, L (1978) *Mind and Society*. Cambridge, Mass: Harvard University Press

Wu, H, Palmer, D and Field, S (2011) Understanding teachers' professional identity and beliefs in the Chinese heritage language school in the USA. *Language, Culture and Curriculum* 24 (1) p47-60

Young, A and Hélot, C (2008) Parent-teacher partnerships: Co-constructing knowledge about languages and cultures in a French primary school. In Kenner, C and Hickey, T (eds)

Index

academic language 56-57
action research 5, 69-73
Ajegbo, K. 95
Al-Azami, S. 53
Anderson, J. 4, 65, 66, 96, 116

Barnhardt, R. 94
Barradas, O. 66
Begum, S. 67
Berryman, M. 94
bilingual learning
    conceptual transfer 29-32, 44-46, 54
    cultural knowledge 38-39, 46-48
    metalinguistic awareness 35-38, 44, 54
translation 32-35, 37, 52, 54
bilingual resource materials 55-56
bilingual literacy development ix, x, 14, 32-34, 41-43, 50-51, 54-55, 92
bilingual numeracy development 30-32, 34-35, 38-39, 57
bilingual strategies 6-7, 52, 56, 59-60, 68, 80-83, 85-88, 91-93
Blackledge, A.   68
Bode, P. 64, 95
Botelho, M. 64
Bourdieu, P. 4
Brock, A. 96

Causley, C. 92
Chen, Y. 30, 66

children's views on bilingual learning 11, 17-20, 22, 27-28, 40-41, 51, 100-102
Chung, Y-C. 66, 116
Clyne, M. 66
Collaborative Learning 30
complementary schools
    assessment 67, 78-79
    curriculum 96-97, 102
    high expectations 77-79
    learning and teaching strategies 6-7, 67-68, 75-76, 79-81
    mainstream teachers' views 61-62, 73-75
    multi-level classes 62, 65
    performance 67, 78
    parents' views 21
    sites 6, 65, 70
    teacher development 65-66, 71, 83-85
    teacher-student interaction 66, 76-79
Conteh, J. 67, 96
Crawford, J. 64
Creese, A. 40, 67, 68
Cruickshank, K. 3
Cummins, J. 4, 30, 40, 65, 95, 96
Curdt-Christiansen, X-L. 67

Dash, P. 63
Datta, M. 38
De Acosta, M. 63
DES 64
DfES 4
Duff, P. 65

Early, M. 40, 96
Edwards, V. 35
Eilers, R. 57
Evans, D. 118

family involvement in learning 43-46, 53-54, 55, 82, 91, 94, 96, 102, 103-105, 113-114
Fernandez, S. 66
Foucault, M. 95
Francis, B. 66

Gillborn, D. 95
Glynn, T. 94
Goldsmiths Multilingual Learning 24, 89, 116
Gregory, E. 30, 62, 63, 65, 67, 80
groupwork 67, 79-80, 83-84

Hall, K. 65, 66, 67, 68, 96
Hawkins, M. 63
Heller, M. 3
Hélot, C. 94
home and community knowledge 11-12, 31, 38-39, 43, 62-64, 92-94, 111-112, 118-119
Hornberger, N. 64

identities x, 3, 20, 23, 40-41, 48-50, 55, 98, 105, 111
independent learning 67, 79-80
Issa, T. 65, 66, 67, 68, 97

Kawagley, O. 94

Kenner, C. 2, 38, 44, 63, 67, 94

kinship terms 8, 11, 39, 46-47, 104-105

Knight, J. 35

Lam, E. 3

learning communities 66, 79-80, 89, 103, 119

learning power xiii, 94, 97, 115, 119

Lee, S. 63

Lemberger, N. 30

Liu, P. 66

Lo Bianco, J. 65

Long, S. 64

McCaffery, J. 65, 96

Martin, P. 65

Martin-Jones, M. 38

May, S. 95

Maylor, U. 68, 96

Moll. L. 94

Monaghan, F. 35

monolingual ideologies 3-4, 23, 64-65, 95

monolingual spaces at school 2, 19

Moore, D. 32

multicultural curriculum 93-97, 103, 105-111, 114-116, 118

multilingualism
at home 2-3, 92
at school 24-25, 51-52, 81-83, 114-116
in the community x, 7, 9, 21-22

NALDIC 30, 56, 60

National Literacy Trust 25

National Resource Centre for Supplementary Education x, 64, 88, 117

Nieto, S. 64, 95

O'Rourke, B. 95

Our Languages x, 64, 68, 117

Pantazi, E. 68

Pearce, S. 95

popular culture 15-16, 48

Robertson, L. 69, 73, 95, 97

Rogoff, B. 62

Rosario-Ramos, E. 3

Rosowsky, A. 67

Ruby, M. 6, 93

Saxena, M. 38

simultaneous worlds 2, 9, 23

Sneddon, R. 24, 35

switching between languages x, 8, 9, 18, 43, 46

Sylheti x, 7-8

Tagore, R. x, 41, 102

teachers' views on bilingual learning 5, 14, 20, 57-58, 73-76, 93, 97-100, 114

Tower Hamlets 4, 57, 69

Tran, A. 66

transliteration 8, 41, 44, 50, 52-55, 82, 92

Tuafuti, P. 65, 96

Valdés, G. 3

Vassie, P. 118

Volk, D. 63, 64

Vygotsky, L. 36, 62, 76

Wang, S. 64

whole-class lessons 51-52

Williams, A. 65

Williams, C. 65, 66, 67, 68, 97

Wu, H. 66, 68, 96

Young, A. 94